Holy Handmaids of the Lord

JULIE ONDERKO

HOLY HANDMAIDS OF THE LORD

Women Saints Who Won the Battle for Souls

SOPHIA INSTITUTE PRESS
Manchester, New Hampshire

Sophia Institute Press
Box 5284, Manchester, NH 03108
1-800-888-9344

www.SophiaInstitute.com

Sophia Institute Press® is a registered trademark of Sophia Institute.

Library of Congress Cataloging-in-Publication Data

Names: Onderko, Julie, author.
Title: Holy handmaids of the Lord : women saints who won the battle for souls / Julie Onderko.
Description: Manchester, New Hampshire : Sophia Institute Press, 2019. |
  Includes bibliographical references. | Summary: "Briefly tells of the
  heroic, holy lives of more than a dozen female Catholic saints,
  including Sts. Perpetua, Monica, Joan, Thérèse, and Faustina"—
  Provided by publisher.
Identifiers: LCCN 2019034971 | ISBN 9781622827213 (paperback)
Subjects: LCSH: Christian women saints—Biography.
Classification: LCC BX4656 .O53 2019 | DDC 282.092/52 [B]—dc23
LC record available at https://lccn.loc.gov/2019034971

First printing

To my daughters-in-law, Rhapsody, Chantelle, and Tareyn: you are all incredible gifts, and I thank God for you. To my granddaughters, my goddaughters, and all future Onderko women who will come into the family through birth, adoption, or marriage — this book is for you!

Always remember who you are: royalty, warrior princesses, and daughters of the Most High God, with all the privileges and responsibilities of such a noble identity.

Contents

Acknowledgments

I believe our Blessed Mother commissioned this work. It took me a while to say yes to her request. This decision needed to be put through a careful discernment process; the subject matter was weighty, the message would probably grate against modern sensibilities, and I wasn't sure if I was up to it. But I was inspired by Jesus' words to Saint Faustina, "Do what you can do, and I will make up for what is lacking in you." And indeed, Our Lord did this for me … through others.

On a practical level, the demands of research and writing take their toll. I simply could not have accomplished this work without the practical support, encouragement, and spiritual backing of my husband, Tom.

Father Giles Dimock, O.P., my spiritual director, helped me to discern this project, reading every word as it was written and counseling me the entire way.

I treasure the insights and suggestions of Theresa Becker. Her unique perspective as a Catholic wife, mother, grandmother, and faithful Catholic woman were invaluable to the construction of this book.

The encouragement given to me by my pastor, Monsignor John Cihak, was truly sustaining. I have benefited from his insights, edits, and instruction. He has taught me so much.

Arlette Popiel responded yes to what the Lord asked—she supported my husband and me as a prayer warrior during the writing of this book.

I am truly grateful to all these friends in Christ as well as those not listed here who have supported me and this work through their prayers and sacrifices.

What on Earth Is Going On?

The earth is a combat zone where souls are won or lost for an eternity. We, the members of Christ's Body here on earth, are called the Church Militant precisely because we are in a battle. The spoils of this war are nothing less than the most valuable thing we possess — our eternal souls.

Jesus was victorious over sin and death, and it is *only* through Jesus that we are redeemed. He is "the way and the truth and the life" (John 14:6). The Lord in His divine wisdom involved others, however, irreplaceably so, in the mystery of salvation. Mary's participation was necessary for Jesus to carry out His mission — the work of our redemption. But we have our part to play as well.

Jesus Christ, the Savior of the world, wants us to partner with Him, His Mother, Saint Joseph, and all the angels and saints, to save the world. We are called to do battle with the infernal foe whose entire purpose is our eternal damnation.

Jesus received His human nature, in which He defeated Satan and redeemed the world, from a woman. Because of this, the devil hates human beings and wants to bring every person he can down to hell with him. Moreover, he has a particular vendetta against the rest of the offspring of "the woman." If we are followers of Christ — that's us.

The dragon became angry with the woman and went off to wage war against the rest of her offspring, those who keep God's commandments and bear witness to Jesus. (Rev. 12:17)

* * *

In the first part of this work, "Holy Women Battling for Souls," we encounter women saints who, in their particular circumstances and vocations, took up the challenge to fight our enemy. In the next part, "We Are Complementary in Mission," we find the beauty and the power of God's plan as men and women together fight the devil and his destructive designs. In the final part, "Mary, the Ultimate Warrior Woman: Her Story and Ours," we consider our human story from its beginning and explore Old Testament women who prefigured the Virgin Mary, the preeminent warrior woman and our greatest advocate. We conclude by pondering God's love for us and our identity in Christ. From this truth we discover, like our elder sisters in Christ, that we, too, have an irreplaceable role in the great drama of human salvation.

Part 1

Holy Women Battling for Souls

Mystic Warrior Perpetua

From the beginning of the Church until the end of time, the devil will continue to wage war against the offspring of the woman — those who keep God's commandments and bear witness to Jesus. Included in the evil serpent's strategy is the demise of a young Roman wife and mother, Perpetua (A.D. 182–203), who converted to Christianity during the reign of Emperor Septimius Severus (A.D. 193–211), a brutal period of persecution in the Church.

In second and third centuries, Roman girls, even those from noble families like Perpetua's, were not usually educated. But because of her father's affection, Perpetua was privileged; she could read and write, and the Church is blessed because we have her prison diary. From it, we learn about her and her companions during their imprisonment. We also come to understand her personal challenges. Perpetua unashamedly shares her mystical experiences, illuminating the spiritual reality of the situation.

We do not know the details of Perpetua's conversion. But we do know that at the time of her arrest, she and her four companions (which included Felicity, a pregnant young slave), were still catechumens, receiving Christian instruction in preparation for the sacrament of Baptism. During the initial phase after the arrest,[1] "while still with the persecutors,"[2] they were baptized. A few days later, they were sent to the dungeon.

The early Church found ways to reach out to and support imprisoned disciples, and for a time Perpetua's father, mother, and brother were able to visit her. From her diary, we can conclude that she came from a loving family and consequently suffered immensely because of the distress that her imprisonment caused them.

The separation from her infant created a particular anguish, a torment unique to motherhood. Since she was breastfeeding, her breasts swelled and she ached for her child: a constant reminder that her baby was hungry. What a torment for any mother to endure! Perpetua does not tell us how she managed it (perhaps a monetary payoff), but she found a way to have her child brought to her. She writes:

> I obtained for my infant to remain in the dungeon with me; immediately I grew strong and was relieved from distress and anxiety about my infant; and the dungeon became to me as it were a palace, so that I preferred being there to being elsewhere.[3]

---

[1] It appears from the diary that during this time, opportunities to recant, or to make the obligatory sacrifice to the Roman gods, were offered. Family came to encourage the Christians to comply with their captors—Perpetua's father did so—before harsher punishments were inflicted or final judgments passed.

[2] Saint Perpetua and Tertullian of Carthage, *Martyrdom of St. Perpetua and St. Felicity and Other Writings*, trans. R. E. Wallis (Philadelphia: Dalcassian Publishing, 2017), 7.

[3] Ibid., 7–8.

All Things Visible and Invisible

In the Nicene Creed, we acknowledge the spiritual world and affirm a belief in God, "the Father almighty, maker of heaven and earth, of all things visible and invisible." There is always more to a situation (the invisible) than what is obvious (the visible). What we do in this life, in this visible world in which we "work out our salvation with fear and trembling" (see Phil. 2:12), has spiritual and eternal consequences. Perpetua was keenly aware of both the material and the immaterial world. She was a mystic.[4] It is understandable, then, that when her brother (who was also a Christian), came to visit her, he asked, "My dear sister, you are already in a position of great dignity, and are such that you may ask for a vision, and that it may be made known to you whatever this is to result in, a passion [martyrdom] or an escape."[5] Perpetua understood that God had given her mystical gifts. She writes, "And I knew that I was privileged to converse with the Lord,"[6] so she asked the Lord to reveal the outcome of her imprisonment and recorded the experience in her diary:

> And I asked, and this was what was shown me. I saw a golden ladder of marvelous height, reaching up even to heaven, and very narrow, so that persons could only ascend it one by one; and on the sides of the ladder was

---

[4] A mystic experiences a unique, extraordinary knowledge and presence of God; it is a gift of grace from God. The mystic can predispose himself to it through love of God and detachment of the world, but it is a total gift. The mystic is often more aware of the unseen realities—both the material (physical) and the immaterial (spiritual) world.

[5] Saint Perpetua and Tertullian, *Martyrdom of St. Perpetua*, 8.

[6] Ibid.

fixed every kind of iron weapon.... And under the ladder itself was crouching a dragon of wonderful size, who
lay in wait for those who ascended, and frightened them
from the ascent. And Saturus went up first ... and turned
towards me, and said to me, "Perpetua, I am waiting for
you; but be careful that the dragon does not bite you."
And I said, "In the name of the Lord Jesus Christ, he
shall not hurt me." And from under the ladder itself, as
if in fear of me, he slowly lifted up his head; and as I trod
upon the first step, I trod upon his head. And I went up.

In the vision, Perpetua ascends the ladder up to heaven and
is welcomed by God and greeted by the saints. From the content
of the vision, she and her brother "understood that it was to be
a passion [martyrdom], and we ceased henceforth to have any
hope in this world."[7]

Pressure from Her Father

During her internment, Perpetua's father visited her with heartfelt
pleading. He did everything in his power to convince Perpetua
to deny her Christianity and come back to her family, appealing
to her motherhood and her child's need as well as Perpetua's
obligation to him in his old age. What daughter's heart would
not be wrenched by such entreaties? She records her father's
words in her diary:

Have pity, my daughter, on my grey hairs. Have pity on
your father, if I am worthy to be called a father by you....
I have preferred you to all your brothers, have regard to

[7] Ibid.

your mother ... have regard to your son, who will not be able to live after you. Lay aside your courage, and do not bring us all to destruction.[8]

His actions, perhaps, spoke louder than words. Perpetua described her father's conduct as he tried to dissuade her from her inevitable end of death in a Roman amphitheater:

These things said my father in his affection, kissing my hands, and throwing himself at my feet; and with tears he called me not Daughter, but Lady. And I grieved over the grey hairs of my father.... When the day of the exhibition drew near, my father, worn with suffering, came in to me [his last visit], and began to tear out his beard ... and to cast himself down on his face ... and to utter words as might move all creation. I grieved."[9]

The little band of believers was taken from the prison to a town-hall-style gathering and given the opportunity to make the obligatory offering to one of the Roman gods, which would secure their release. In this public setting, Perpetua's father came with Perpetua's infant son in his arms and begged her to "offer sacrifice for the well-being of the emperors." She refused. What happened next led to the condemnation of her and her companions. "Are you Christian?" the procurator asked. "I am Christian," came her reply and her friends answered in kind. Perpetua relates:

The Procurator then delivers judgment on all of us, and condemns us to the wild beasts, and we went down

[8]   Ibid., 8–9.
[9]   Ibid., 9.

9

cheerfully to the dungeon. [From this point onward, Perpetua's infant was no longer brought to her in prison.] And even as God willed it, the child no longer desired the breast, nor did my breast cause me uneasiness, lest I should be tormented by care for my babe.[10]

Felicity

Christian love does not differentiate between social class. Saint Paul writes to the Christians in Galatia:

> For all of you who were baptized into Christ have clothed yourselves with Christ. There is neither Jew nor Greek, there is neither slave nor free person, there is not male and female; for you are all one in Christ Jesus. (Gal. 3:27–28)

Felicity was a slave and was pregnant at the time of her arrest. Yet the respectably born and educated Perpetua saw Felicity not as a slave, which was her status in society, but as her sister and equal in Christ. Felicity, too, possessed mystical gifts that were recognized by Perpetua, who wrote, "to her [Felicity] also the Lord's favor approached in the same way."[11]

Felicity relied heavily on her Christian friends, for her biggest fear was facing her execution alone, without them; and it was the likely outcome. Pregnant women were not part of Roman public exhibitions, and she was already eight months along. Her sentence would be carried out after she gave birth. The companions prayed that she would deliver before their execution day, "lest she should

---

[10] Ibid.
[11] Ibid., 13.

shed her sacred and guiltless blood among some who had been wicked." We can only imagine the depth of their friendship and their desire to travel the path of martyrdom together. Fortunately, Felicity delivered her child in time. Perpetua reports that "thus she brought forth a little girl, which a certain sister brought up as a daughter."[12]

The Head of the Serpent

In another vision granted the day before the exhibition, the eternal perspective of her struggle was shown to Perpetua. The saints in heaven called to her, "Perpetua, we are waiting for you; come!"[13] Again, Perpetua was confirmed that her battle was indeed with the devil, and for a second time in her mystical vision, she "trod upon his head."[14]

The bruising (crushing) of the head of the serpent is a recurring theme with warrior women, prefiguring the Virgin Mary throughout salvation history, and it occurs explicitly in Perpetua's first and last vision.[15] That connection was not lost on the early Church Fathers. Saint Augustine of Hippo (354–430) draws attention to it in a sermon:

> The dragon therefore was trodden down by the chaste foot and victorious tread of the blessed Perpetua, when that upward ladder was shown her whereby she should go to God; and the head of the ancient serpent, which to

[12] Ibid., 13–14.
[13] Ibid., 11.
[14] Ibid.
[15] Ibid.

her that fell was a stumbling, was made a step unto her that rose.[16]

The head of the dragon, the thing created by the devil to dissuade souls from making the ascent to God, became in fact, Perpetua's stepping-stone to heaven. What Satan contrives for our downfall, God uses for our victory. It has backfired on the him since the beginning in the Garden of Eden. In this way, God humiliates Satan, turning Satan's own work against him.

The devil threw all he had at Jesus, and from a worldly perspective it appeared as though Jesus was defeated on that Roman Cross. Yet we know that the Crucifixion was the definitive victory over mankind's greatest enemy: death. Until the end of time, the followers of Christ will continue to use the devil's own weapons against him. This is an invisible, spiritual reality that must be seen through the eyes of faith. What appears to be lost or defeated by the design of the evil one does not have to be so. Have faith — the victory belongs to Christ!

"The Day of Their Victory Shone Forth"[17]

The Christians were led from the prison to the amphitheater, where each gave a final witness before the crowd. Remarkably, the account describes the Christians as joyful. Perpetua and Felicity "stripped and clothed with nets, were led forth. The populace

---

[16] Saint Augustine, *The Passions of Sts. Perpetua and Felicity*, MM, *A New Edition and Translation of the Latin Text, Together with the Sermons of St. Augustine upon These Saints* (London: Sheed and Ward, 1931), 46.

[17] Saint Perpetua and Tertullian, *Martyrdom of St. Perpetua*, 14.

shuddered as they saw one young woman of delicate frame, and another with breasts still dropping from recent childbirth."

The women were tossed about by a "savage cow,"[18] while the others were made sport of by various means for the spectators. When the crowd had had enough, they called for the sword. The valiant disciples "first kissed one another, that they might consummate their martyrdom with a kiss of peace. The rest indeed, immovable and in silence, received the sword-thrust," as did Perpetua. But it did not kill her, and the executioner was visibly shaken. She therefore assisted him: "She herself placed the wavering right hand of the youthful gladiator to her throat."[19]

For the early Church, whose members bore the weight of horrific persecution, the martyrdoms of Perpetua, Felicity, and their companions was truly fortifying. To this day, we are spiritually enriched, inspired, and encouraged by their ultimate witness.

> The Church has painstakingly collected the records of those who persevered to the end in witnessing to their faith. These are the acts of the Martyrs. They form the archives of truth written in letters of blood. (CCC 2474)

---

[18] Ibid., 39.
[19] Ibid., 15–16.

2

A Young Teen Battles for a Soul: Thérèse of Lisieux

Guilty! The year was 1887, and Henri Pranzini had been convicted of three murders: a high-end prostitute, her maid, and the maid's twelve-year-old daughter. Their throats slit—shocking news in all of France. Henri Pranzini was incarcerated in La Roquette prison, where his death sentence would be carried out under the blade of the guillotine.

Pranzini was a sophisticated fellow. Born in Egypt, he was an educated man and spoke eight languages. He was well traveled, with an assortment of unique life experiences, including interpreting for both the Russian and British armies. But when he arrived in Paris, rumors were that he was penniless.[20] He became a professional blackmailer and was known to have a way with women, targeting the wealthy in order to learn their incriminating secrets for his financial gain.

---

[20] K. V. Turley, "The Killer and the Saint: Pranzini and Thérèse," *Catholic World Report*, October 1, 2017, https://www.catholic-worldreport.com/2017/10/01/the-killer-and-the-saint-pranzini-and-therese/.

The maxim "real life is stranger than fiction" is proved true in the life of Pranzini. Who would conceive a story in which his eternal destiny would be determined by a teenage girl he did not know and would never meet in this life?

Fourteen-year-old Marie Françoise-Thérèse Martin (Saint Thérèse of Lisieux, 1873–1897), lived a relatively sheltered life, though she did know hardship, having lost her mother when she was only four years old. But she was the youngest, and so her older sisters took on the role of mother, doting on her and spoiling her in many ways. She did not learn to do some of the basic things most girls learn in the home. For instance, Thérèse did not perform any of the household chores, nor was she able to manage the brushing and styling of her own hair; there was always a willing older sister to do it for her.

This young teen exuded innocence and used flowery speech that would be a challenge for someone in the twenty-first century to take seriously. For example, her father, Louis (who never remarried after his wife died) was her "king," and she was his "queen." In the very childish-sounding exchanges between Thérèse and her father, she was absolutely genuine, earnest, and innocent—like a child. Jesus said, "Let the children come to me, and do not prevent them; for the kingdom of heaven belongs to such as these" (Matt. 19:14). In reading Thérèse, it benefits us to persevere even when the language's childlike quality may put us off. On a closer examination we find a theological depth that can often escape the learned and experienced. According to Pope John Paul II, "The insights of faith expressed in her [Thérèse's] writings are so vast and profound that they deserve a place among the great spiritual masters."[21]

---

[21] John Paul II, Proclamation of St. Thérèse of the Child Jesus and the Holy Face as a "Doctor of the Church," October 19, 1997.

At a young age, Thérèse knew she had a vocation to the religious life, specifically to the Carmelite Order. She was consumed with a desire to save the most hardened of sinners and spiritually "birth" them into God's kingdom. To do this, she invoked heavenly help, not considering the possibility of winning heaven for sinners as modeled by the "great saints," such as Teresa of Avila or John of the Cross, who exemplified heroic prayer and sacrifices. Rather she was intuitive with her childlike trust in Jesus and believed that a divine strategy of love would open heaven's gates. She writes:

> My protectors in heaven and my privileged ones ... are those who have stolen it [heaven], such as the Holy Innocents [the children killed by royal decree when king Herod learned of the Messiah's birth in Bethlehem] and the good thief [who hung on a cross beside Jesus and asked Him to remember him when He came into His kingdom]. The great Saints gained heaven through their works [i.e., Teresa of Avila and John of the Cross]. As for me, I want to follow the example of the thieves: I want to gain it through ruse, a subterfuge of love that will open its entrance, to me and to the poor sinners.[22]

It is noteworthy that Thérèse is not only a canonized saint, but also a Doctor of the Church. Those whom the Church names Doctors have a unique charism or gift, contributing something specifically significant to the Church and the world. In the two millennia of Church history, only thirty-six Doctors have been named, and Thérèse is among them.

---

[22] *The Complete Thérèse of Lisieux*, trans. and ed. Robert J. Edmonson, C.J. (Brewster, MA: Paraclete Press, 2009), 273.

In her autobiography, she writes about the rich who have elevators in their homes and do not need to climb the stairs. She knows she is "too little" to perform any substantial deeds or make any lofty climbs, so she sets about to find a spiritual elevator, the fastest way to holiness. " I would also like to find an elevator to lift me up to Jesus, because I'm too little to climb the rough staircase of perfection."[23] She also does this on behalf of others.

The way of ascent is simple: love. Love gives potency to any minuscule offering. Doing all things, no matter how insignificant they may appear, with great love for Jesus *is* that spiritual elevator. In essence, this is St. Thérèse's "little way."

This doctrine is illustrated in Henri Pranzini's story. At the time of Pranzini's conviction, Thérèse was a young teen still living at home. And although her father, Louis, tried to shelter his youngest daughter, he could not keep the sensational news about the nefarious Pranzini from reaching her. Nor could he have imagined that Thérèse, his innocent little "queen," was honing her spiritual skills as a Christian warrior—her intent to enter the battlefield for the soul of this killer. Thérèse's response is notable:

> I heard about a terrible criminal who had just been condemned to death for some horrible crimes. Everything would lead one to believe that he would die without repenting. I wanted at all cost to prevent him from going to hell. In order to do that I used every imaginable means: Sensing that in myself I could do nothing, I offered to God all the infinite merits of Our Lord and the treasures of the Holy Church.... Deep in my heart I felt certainty that our desires would be granted, but in order

---

[23]   Ibid., 184.

to give myself courage to continue to pray for sinners, I told God that I was quite sure that He would forgive poor miserable Pranzini, and that I would believe this even if he did not confess and showed no sign of repentance, so much did I have confidence in Jesus' infinite mercy, but I asked Him only for "a sign" of repentance simply for my consolation.[24]

Pranzini would be Thérèse's test case. Although she was confident of Jesus' mercy and "deep in my heart I felt certainty that our desires would be granted," she asked for a sign. As the spirituality of her little way developed, Thérèse simply wanted confirmation that she was on the correct path.

During Pranzini's internment and execution, Father Jean-Baptiste Faure served as the chaplain at La Roquette Prison. He visited with Pranzini, who was cordial and accepting of the priest's company. But no matter how persuasive the good father was, Pranzini would not make his peace with God and refused Confession. Faithful to the end, Father Faure accompanied Pranzini to his execution. In his book, *Souvenirs de la Roquette: au pied de l'échafaud* (Memories of la Roquette: at the foot of the scaffold), we find Father Faure's account of Pranzini's last moments on this earth:

> When, after saying a last farewell, I took a step back, he cried out in a voice choked with anguish, in a cry full of repentance and faith: "Father, bring me the crucifix!" I quickly went to him and pressed the crucifix to his lips—he kissed it fervently. We exchanged a couple of

[24] Ibid., 86–87.

words.... He was pushed against the platform, a noise sounded, the blade fell ... it was all over.[25]

Solidly confirmed in her little way, fourteen-year-old Thérèse claimed Pranzini as her "first child." She writes:

> The day after his execution I put my hand on the newspaper.... Pranzini had not confessed; he had climbed up onto the scaffold ... when suddenly, gripped with a sudden inspiration, he turned back, grabbed a Crucifix that the priest was holding up to him, and kissed its sacred wounds three times ... the lips of "my first child" were pressed upon the sacred wounds!!!... What an expressibly sweet reply![26]

Thérèse did not focus on her opponent, Satan, or her motivation—she "wanted at all costs to prevent him from going to hell."[27] Rather, Thérèse's attention was focused on Jesus and how much she loved and trusted Him.

It can seem peculiar, awesome, and wondrous to consider that, in a certain sense, Jesus is held captive by our love and trust in Him. Our desire for the salvation of others comes from Him in the first place. He desires that we partner with Him in the ongoing work of salvation. This is a mystery, an incredible privilege, and a tremendous responsibility. And Thérèse, with her childlike confidence in the mercy of God, is a perfect model of this partnership with the Savior.

---

[25] Jean-Baptiste Faure, *Souvenirs de la Roquette: au pied de l'échafaud* (Paris: M. Dreyfous et M. Dalsace, 1896), 142–144. Translated from French to English using Google Translate.

[26] *The Complete Thérèse of Lisieux*, 86.

[27] Ibid.

What an incredible faith-filled disciple we find in Thérèse! Here's a girl who, for her day and time, was about as powerless as any person could be, and yet she put her trust in Jesus, battled Satan for a soul—a multiple murderer no less—and won![28]

---

[28] Of course, we know that Thérèse did not do the saving; Jesus and only Jesus is the Savior. But she did her part, and Pranzini was moved to repentance, appealing to the Crucified Christ in the last moments of his life.

3

Spiritual Motherhood: Monica

Monica (331–387) was praying in the chapel of Blessed Cyprian, awaiting her son Augustine's return. They planned to sail for Rome along with Augustine's mistress and his son, Monica's grandson. The four of them had traveled to the foreign port city from the family home in North Africa. It was a bold move, considering the uncertain times of the mid-fourth-century Roman world, but Augustine believed that his future was in Rome, and Monica had convinced him to bring her along—or so she thought.

In Augustine's *Confessions* we read what happened:

> I deceived her [Monica] and pretended that I had a friend whom I could not leave until he had a fair wind to set sail. Thus I told a lie to my mother—such a wonderful mother—and got away.... I persuaded her with much difficulty to remain for that night in a place near our ship where there was an oratory of Blessed Cyprian. That same night I stole away, but she remained there praying.... The wind blew and swelled our sails and carried us out of sight of the shore, where she in the morning was overwhelmed

with grief, and with her complaints and sighs filled Your [God's] ears."[29]

Monica was by herself in a foreign city. Dealing with the logistics, such as where to stay, how to travel safely, how to maneuver in an unfamiliar city with foreign customs, and so forth, would have been very frightening, especially for a woman alone. More poignant for her would have been the sting of cruel deception. Her son had purposely abandoned her in what was a potentially dangerous situation. Yet Monica would rise to the occasion. Her life to this point had prepared her for it.

Monica was born in Thagaste, North Africa (modern-day Algeria). The family's maidservant, who was quite elderly and had taken care of Monica's father when he was a boy, was a Christian. She remembered the persecutions of the Church when it had been illegal to be a Christian. Through this faithful family servant, Monica came to a deep faith in Jesus Christ. The old woman could never have envisioned that her influence over the spiritual development of young Monica would have such an impact on the course of human history.

When Monica was about thirteen years old, her marriage was arranged with a pagan man, Patricius. As was the custom of the time, she went to live with her husband's family. They were not Christian, and her mother-in-law vehemently disliked her, but Monica eventually won the family's respect and her mother-in-law's affection. In time, Patricius and Monica set up their own household and had three children, two boys and a girl. Monica was about twenty-three when she gave birth to her firstborn, Augustine.

---

[29] *Confessions of Saint Augustine* (Totowa, NJ: Catholic Book Publishing, 1997), 125–126.

Monica never forgot the lessons she learned from her child-hood maidservant, and she practiced her Faith loyally despite the opposition of her husband and his family. This included going to the church twice a day, presumably for morning and evening prayer and perhaps instruction; daily Mass was not celebrated at that time. Monica nurtured her faith and grew in virtue even with less-than-ideal circumstances at home. Her character was noticed and respected. Neighbors consulted with her over disputes and disagreements because she never participated in gossip; their confidences were safe with Monica.

Patricius was not what would be considered "good husband material." He was a pagan, unfaithful to the marriage, and when he drank, he became violent. He did, however, materially provide for the family and saw to the education of his children. For Augustine, who was something of a child prodigy, this meant procuring a sponsor to pay for the gifted youth's higher education. So, arrangements were made, and the seventeen-year-old Augustine headed for the bustling metropolis of Carthage, modern-day Tunisia.

Patricius died while Augustine was away at school. A year before his death, he converted; Monica's prayers on his behalf had been answered. Indeed, Monica made clear her wish that when she died, she be buried next to him. This is not exactly the desire one would expect of a woman finally free of an abusive marriage, but it is a testament of the patient love that Monica had for her convert husband.

After five years away at school, Augustine returned home with a mistress and his young son, Adeodatus. Augustine was educated in rhetoric and very full of himself, having discarded the Faith of his childhood. Much to Monica's disappointment, he had become a follower of Manichaeism, a very fashionable movement at the time.[30] Being skilled in persuasion, Augustine began to influence his younger siblings. Monica, who had been willing to have Augustine with his mistress and her grandson in the home, was now compelled to kick her arrogant son out of the house. She could not have him spreading this poisonous heresy in her own home with her teenage son and daughter there.

His expulsion from the home was short-lived. Monica had a dream of her son's return to the Faith. She took this as a sign and confirmation that she would play a part in how this would work out. With his illegitimate family, Augustine once again moved back into his mother's home.

As time went on, Monica's other children grew up firm in the Faith and were settled to her satisfaction. Augustine still was not. He was however, growing restless and dissatisfied with the local employment opportunities and decided he would go to Rome. Monica believed that he was taking her with him. Instead, she found herself alone and abandoned in a foreign port city. What may appear to be a defeat, however, our Lord can use as part of the coming triumph (see Rom. 8:28). Augustine realized this years later and said of his mother: "She did not know how much joy You [God] would bring her by allowing me to depart from her."[31]

It may sound dysfunctional and even obsessive, but Monica did not return home to Thagaste as we might expect. Rather, she sailed after Augustine. Traveling was not easy in those days. Passenger ships were not a part of the ancient world. Travelers went by merchant vessels as part of the cargo, enduring a great deal of discomfort, extremely unsanitary conditions, and sometimes

---

[30] Manichaeism is a heretical belief that the flesh is bad and only the spirit is good.

[31] *Confessions*, 126.

danger. During Monica's voyage to Rome, the ship encountered a big storm and the crew was frightened, but Monica was certain they would arrive safely. Her firm faith in God gave hope to the passengers and the crew.

When she arrived in Rome, Augustine was not there. He had gone to Milan. Monica again found herself alone in a foreign city. This surely must have tested her faith and made her reexamine the mission that God had given her. *Was her future really tied up in Augustine's conversion? Should she finally let him go, knowing that if he did not change his ways, his soul was destined for eternal separation from God? Would the soul of her son be forever in the grip of the devil?*

Monica set off for Milan. Once there, she took up with the local Christians being shepherded by Bishop Ambrose, a man of keen intelligence, strong faith, and outstanding communication skills. Monica realized that Bishop Ambrose was perhaps the only man on earth who could match Augustine's skill in rhetoric. Surely the bishop could convince Augustine of the truth of Jesus Christ and the Catholic Church. Monica tried to orchestrate her son's conversion. Augustine later wrote:

> He [Ambrose] became annoyed with her persistent entreaty and said to her, "Go on your way and continue in your life of prayer, for it cannot be that a son of such tears should perish." As she many times afterward told me, she received those words as if they had sounded forth from Heaven.[32]

Indeed, as Monica had hoped, Ambrose was able to debate with Augustine and demonstrate that Christianity was the truth

---

[32] Ibid., 84.

he had been seeking. But Augustine was attached to a life of sinful habits — especially those of the flesh. His famous line, "Lord, make me chaste, but not yet," sums up his struggle. He wanted to embrace the truth, but he did not want to relinquish his life of sin. When that moment of grace arrived, Augustine finally gave his will to God and found his heart's desire. The first thing he did was tell his mother!

Augustine's theological teachings and his personal story, *The Confessions*, have been a treasure for the Church through the centuries. The influence of this great sinner turned saint on the Church continues to this day, guiding us in our understanding of theology and our human nature. God had a plan for him, and Monica was most definitely part of that plan, as Augustine himself testifies:

> Could You [God], by Whose grace she was such, despise and reject her tears with which she did not beg of You gold or silver, or any fading and perishable good, but the salvation of her son's soul? Never, oh Lord! But You were present and heard her, and You granted her request, according to the plan that You had designed.[33]

Monica did not live long after Augustine's conversion. As she was dying, her two sons shared their plan to return her body to Thagaste to be buried next to her husband. But Monica had changed. Her path of endurance and testing had done something she did not expect; it had transformed her into a saint. Monica realized that her burial place was trivial. "Nothing is far from God," was her response. She did however, ask for something: "This only I ask, that you will remember me at the Lord's altar

---

[33] Ibid., 128.

wherever you may be." She was fifty-six when she died. Augustine wept freely.

Prayer is the weapon of choice for mothers who are moved by a fierce love for their children. Love drives a mother and compels her to act. A mother is tenacious; she does not give up when it comes to the salvation of her children. She disregards her own status, comfort, and limitations as she confronts Satan for the souls of her children. There is nothing quite like a mother's love.

This is exactly why Jesus shares His own Mother with us. She is our mom, too; we need her, and Satan fears her. The Virgin Mary is the preeminent warrior mother. She is our example, our guide, and our companion in the war for the souls of our children and our spiritual children.

Spiritual Motherhood

God's rescue mission for all humanity required one woman's yes — Mary's fiat: "Behold, I am the handmaid of the Lord. May it be done to me according to your word" (Luke 1:38). Amazing as it sounds, all women, through the gift of femininity, are invited to share the role of spiritual motherhood with Mother Mary. Our fiat to the Lord's invitation puts our unique nature at His service. We see in our bodies, which were created to bring forth life, a physical sign of the character of our souls. We are designed to be receptive, life-giving, humble, tenacious, and nurturing; the Virgin Mary is the archetype. Each woman, in her unique response to God in her feminine nature, has a particular position in His plan to save the world.

Spiritual motherhood is not restricted by circumstances, because it comes through a woman's soul. Biological motherhood is not a requirement for spiritual motherhood. A woman can be single, married, or a religious sister. She can be very young or very old. It does not matter—all women are called to spiritual motherhood.

Young Thérèse Martin understood this. She knew that her feminine receptivity to whatever God had in mind for her would bear spiritual fruit—namely, souls for heaven, spiritual children. Her first "child" was Pranzini, a convicted murderer, a man more than twice her age, someone she had never corresponded with and would never meet. Pranzini was clueless about her existence. His awareness of her initiative was not necessary. Thérèse cooperated with her own feminine nature, as young as she was, to respond to the prompting of the Holy Spirit. She knew that, with Jesus, she could move heaven and earth and the heart of a murderer. This young saint in the making gave her fiat to the Lord and embraced her spiritual maternity—and Pranzini will have all eternity to thank her.[34]

During her life, Saint Thérèse of Lisieux read and reread a book that had a tremendous impactful on the development of her spirituality: *The End of the Present World and the Mysteries of the Future Life*, by the renowned French priest and preacher Father Charles Arminjon. She stated in her autobiography that "reading this book was one of the greatest graces of my life." In it we find a prime example of a mother's role for the souls of her children. Father Arminjon writes:

> He [the child] will know that, next to God, it was the tears, prayers and sighs of that mother which brought about his salvation. "Oh mother," he will exclaim, "I used to love you because you gave me earthly life and provided

---

[34] See St. Thérèse of Lisieux, *The Story of a Soul*, chap. 3.

for my food and my childhood needs; now I love you a thousand times more tenderly, because of the eternal life I have received."[35]

Father Arminjon acknowledges the physical life received from a mother but notes that it is the eternal life received for which the child loves his mother "a thousand times more tenderly." He draws attention to the spiritual motherhood of Saint Monica, who is credited by her son as having "conceived him twice":

O new and happy Monicas, how great your triumphs and joys will be, when you see yourselves surrounded by a whole circle of children whose glory you have secured ...!

Spiritual maternity is the birthright of every Christian woman. It is how we join Mary in her role as warrior mother—snatching souls out of Satan's grip and birthing them into the Kingdom of God.

[35]   Father Charles Arminjon, *The End of the Present World and the Mysteries of the Future Life* (Manchester, NH: Sophia Institute Press, 2008), 229.

4

Holy Quester Joan of Arc

There is something exceptional about persons who give their entire existence to a single quest. If their mission is from God, and if they have responded totally and without reservation, there is no deterring them. They find the means, sometimes in unconventional ways, to follow the inspirations given to them. They could be rightfully called "holy questers," but we more commonly know them as saints.

"I am not afraid; I was born to do this." These are the words of one of these holy questers, Joan of Arc (1412–1431). Her mission from God was to drive the English from occupied French territory and to free France. The obstacles were enormous for anyone. For Joan, it seemed impossible. She was a simple, uneducated peasant girl in fifteenth-century France. But her mission *was* from God and "nothing is impossible with God" (see Luke 1:37; Mark 10:27).

Joan was frequently visited by three saints, from whom she received her instructions: Michael the Archangel, Catherine of Alexandria, and Margaret of Antioch. These three were perfectly suited to assist Joan's mission: Saint Michael, because he was the heavenly warrior, and Saints Catherine and Margaret, who were both young virgin martyrs from the early fourth century. "These heavenly voices taught her to be devout—to go to Mass often, to pray—and ... they enjoined her to save France."[36]

Joan's voices instructed her to speak to Charles VII (1403–1461), known as the Dauphin, the title given to the eldest son of the French king and heir to the throne. Upon her first request made to Charles's general, Joan was turned away and told that her father should give her a whipping. Her second attempt, which involved a demonstration of divine knowledge, resulted in a meeting. But Charles was wary. Before her arrival, he disguised himself, setting another man in his place to pose as the Dauphin. When Joan entered the court, she walked directly to Charles, and despite the disguise, acknowledged his true identity. This display of her mystical gifts as well as a private conversation with Charles, convinced him as to the authenticity of her mission.

This opened the doors she was seeking. Before long, Joan was mounted on a high-spirited charger with her standard, bearing the names of the King and Queen of Heaven, "Jesus, Maria," held high for her troops to see as she led them into one victorious battle after another. What this young Christian warrior accomplished was truly extraordinary: a teenage peasant girl successfully leading a French army in driving the English off occupied French lands. And, as her voices had instructed, she saw Charles VII crowned king of France.

Maintaining the religious integrity of the mission was a priority for Joan. Her troops were to be spiritually prepared for battle. She encouraged them to confess, pray, and frequent the sacraments. It was common practice for groups of prostitutes to follow military bands, but Joan would have none of it. With sword in

---

[36] Siobhan Nash-Marshall, *Joan of Arc: A Spiritual Biography* (New York: Crossroads Publishing, 1999), 39.

hand, she personally drove them away. Fighting was not allowed on Sundays, no matter the perceived military advantage. The exception was made only in purely defensive situations.[37] In the direst of circumstances, when Joan was badly wounded, taking an arrow in the shoulder near her neck, she refused a charm offered to her, saying, "I would rather die than do what I know to be a sin or to be against God's law."[38]

Before Joan's leadership, the French did not believe they could resist the English and in some territories had not. Apathy and despondency had replaced the will to fight; they had no leader who could inspire them. With Joan, the country began to believe they could have a future free from English domination. Joan's fervor and belief in victory were contagious. More than once, when the French were forced into retreat, Joan would charge ahead, a lone warrior against the odds, which inspired her army to follow her back into the fight and to an unexpected victory. Faith is powerful and attractive. Joan was confident. Trusting in the Lord, she proclaimed, "I am sent here by God, the King of Heaven." Little wonder that volunteers flocked to join her army.

Despite her popularity, her magnetism, and her ability to gather loyal troops for the cause of France, political influences were orchestrated to undermine her efforts; jealousy, suspicion, and maneuvering were at work. Despite her miraculous accomplishments, not everyone believed that Joan had been commissioned by the Lord. When she was captured in battle,[39] Charles VII, who had obtained his crown because of her efforts, did not

---

[37] Ibid., 79.

[38] Ibid., 78.

[39] High-profile prisoners were held by the feudal lord of whoever had captured the prisoner.

pay the customary ransom. Charles's advisers had convinced him that Joan "had fallen out of favor with God."[40] She was sold to the English and imprisoned. Charles may as well have ordered her execution.

Not only did the English want Joan dead; they also wanted her discredited by attributing her successes to the devil, not to God. If Joan lost her credibility, they could then assert that Charles's claim to the throne of France was brought about by evil means and, therefore, not legitimate. To accomplish this, Joan needed to be tried in an ecclesiastical court. The bishop of Beauvais, having been ousted from English-occupied France by Joan's army, had a personal vendetta against her. He was happy to comply with the English plot.

During her unjust trial, in which the verdict was decided prior to the proceedings, she answered the questions simply and directly. With blunt honesty she protested the injustice of her treatment and warned those who judged her:

> I do not dare take off these leggings, or wear them if they are not tightly laced. You both know that my jailers have tried to do violence to me several times....
>
> Be careful, you who call yourself my judge! Be careful about what you are doing. Because my quest does come from God, and you are taking a terrible risk.[41]

Joan was unshakable. For all the efforts to wear her down, her accusers could not trip her up. Regardless of the straightforward and simple brilliance of her answers, her judges were all in

---

[40] Barbara Calamari and Sandra DiPasqua, *Ancient and Modern Saints* (New York: Viking Studio, 2007), 111.

[41] Ibid., 137, 148.

agreement—if Joan did not retract her statements, she would be burned at the stake.

Up to this point in her short career as a military leader, Joan had been fearless, keeping her focus on the mission. But for her, the situation in the English prison was torturous. Since it was an ecclesiastic trial, Joan legally should have been imprisoned in a convent and watched over by women. Instead she was illegally incarcerated in an English prison, and men were her guards. And for the first time since she took up arms, Joan was dreadfully alone in a hostile environment where she was chained at the ankles and the neck and in constant fear of being raped. She was without the spiritual support of the sacraments. Moreover, Joan was terrified of burning: "I would far rather have my head chopped off seven times over, than be burned!" The English prison was Joan's Gethsemane.

Under this unimaginable pressure, the young warrior's resolve waned. Joan faltered and signed the retraction—but only temporarily. In the end, this young warrior woman would rather face death by burning than deny God His rightful place in her life.

Fiat: Our Total Gift of Self to God

Many saints have hoped for the opportunity to spill their blood in imitation of Our Lord Jesus Christ. Among them we find Thérèse of Lisieux, who had been inspired by Joan along her own path to sainthood. In Thérèse's autobiography, *The Story of a Soul,* we read:

> Like Thee, O Adorable Spouse, I would be scourged, I would be crucified! I would be flayed like St. Bartholomew, plunged into boiling oil like St. John, or, like St. Ignatius

of Antioch, ground by the teeth of wild beasts into a bread worthy of God. With St. Agnes and St. Cecilia, I would offer my neck to the sword of the executioner, and like St. Joan of Arc I would murmur the name of Jesus at the stake.[42]

The Lord does not offer martyrdom to most of us, but He does ask for our hearts, our love, our wills—essentially our total fiat. Giving our fiat to Jesus is, for most of us, a process; it is a kind of martyrdom because it is a dying to ourselves. "Putting on the mind of Christ" (see Phil: 2:5) is a spiritual journey taken one trustful step at a time.

Joan's fiat is what made her a saint and a holy quester. All of us are called to the same radical commitment. It will, of course, manifest itself differently for each of us. We have only to look at the lives of the saints and see the extensive variety found there. But the common qualifier—that one thing shared by all who attain sainthood—is an uncompromising yes to God.

---

[42] St. Thérèse of Lisieux, *The Story of a Soul*, chap. 11.

5

Knight and Feeble Maid:
Maria Faustina Kowalska

Maria Faustina Kowalska (1905–1938) believed that she had a religious vocation, but her parents did not approve; she was needed to contribute to the family welfare. They were poor peasants living in Glogowiec, Poland. Faustina was one of ten children and had received only three years of primary education. So, at fourteen years old, she went to work as a housekeeper.

During her eighteenth year, she again made an earnest appeal to her parents to let her enter a convent, and again they refused. Faustina suppressed her calling until one pivotal night.

She was at a dance with her sister and some companions when everything in the room suddenly fell away from her senses and she saw only Jesus. He asked her, "How long shall I put up with you and how long will you keep putting Me off?"[43] When the room returned to normal, Faustina slipped out of the dance unnoticed and went directly to the Cathedral of Saint Stanislaus Kostka:

[43] Saint Maria Faustina Kowalska, *Diary: Divine Mercy in My Soul* (Stockbridge, MA: Marian Press, 2000), no. 9.

It was almost twilight; there were only a few people in the cathedral. Paying no attention to what was happening around me, I fell prostrate before the Blessed Sacrament and begged the Lord to be good enough to give me to understand what I should do next. Then I heard these words: "Go at once to Warsaw; you will enter a convent there."[44]

Jesus asks everything of us. If He really is who He says He is, then we owe Him ourselves, completely. This may sound harsh and demanding, but Jesus first gives us Himself—totally. Love demands totality, and Divine Love asks nothing else but the entire gift of self in response. Jesus shed His blood—all of it—for us. While hanging on the Cross He gave us His Mother—*withholding nothing for Himself*. His is a full, absolute donation of love. This is a mystery. And in this exchange, we receive unimaginable blessings.

But even so, giving ourselves to Christ is *still* difficult for us because we are fallen and weak. It is a sacrifice that requires a leap of faith. If we were in Faustina's position, would we leave home and family to go to a big city where we don't know anyone? Would we do this, knowing there was no way to get back home if things did not go well? It's one thing to ponder what we might do in a certain situation, but it's quite another to ask a legitimate question at this moment: *Will I allow the expectations of others to write the story of my life, or will I ask Jesus what His plan is for me?*

Faustina was penniless, uneducated, and without connections in Warsaw. She left home in secret and without her parents' blessing. She walked away from all the earthly security she knew to respond to Jesus' call. She writes:

[44] Ibid., no. 10.

I rose from prayer, came home, and took care of things that needed to be settled. As best I could, I confided to my sister what took place within my soul. I told her to say good-bye to our parents, and thus, in my one dress, with no other belongings, I arrived in Warsaw. When I got off the train and saw that all were going their separate ways, I was overcome with fear. What am I to do? To whom should I turn, as I know no one? So I said to the Mother of God, "Mary, lead me, guide me." Immediately I heard words within me telling me to leave the town and to go to a certain nearby village where I would find a safe lodging for the night. I did so and found, in fact, that everything was just as the Mother of God told me.[45]

This was the first step of faith-filled surrender that would lead to Faustina's consecrated life as a bride of Christ. And from the very beginnings of her journey, she understood her identity as a warrior and concerned herself with that reality. She writes of her soul:

It must now look upon things differently from what it had up to now. It does not seek reassurance in a false peace, but makes ready for battle. It knows it comes from a warrior race. It is now much more aware of everything. It knows that it is of royal stock. It is concerned with all that is great and holy.[46]

By most earthly standards, Faustina Kowalska was a nobody, just a simple Polish nun. But she knew her true identity in Christ; she was from royal stock and therefore a princess—a *warrior*

[45] Ibid., nos. 9–11.
[46] Ibid., no. 120.

princess. She understood what her life was about and concerned herself with *all that is great and holy*. And like so many of us, she struggled with accepting her mission; "when I became aware of God's great plans for me, I was frightened at their greatness and felt myself quite incapable of fulfilling them."[47]

Divine Mercy for Our Times

The human family has been through, and continues to live in, very wicked times. Our world, in many ways, is a wreck. Consider the wars, including two worldwide wars that have plagued the peoples of the earth these last hundred years. Persecutions and martyrdoms have never in Christian history reached the crescendo that twentieth-century Christians have suffered, and it continues. The number of abortions worldwide is simply staggering, hundreds of millions to date. We are disordered. As a human race we are a perverted version of what we should be. Most men and women do not know who they are or why they are here. Our world is broken.

The devil appears to have had his way with us and seems to have fashioned a great harvest of souls for himself in the process. But God is never outdone by evil. St. Paul reminds us, "Where sin increases, grace abounds all the more" (see Rom. 5:20). The message of Divine Mercy is God's hope-filled response to our damaged, hurting, sinful day and age. And He chose an unlikely warrior as His messenger in this battle for souls. Jesus explained to Faustina, "In the Old Covenant I sent prophets wielding thunderbolts to My people. Today I am sending you with My mercy to the people of the whole world."[48]

---

[47] Ibid., no. 429.
[48] Ibid., no. 1588.

Through mystical experiences, Jesus repeatedly taught Faustina how to appropriate His mercy to the world. In the first vision, St. Faustina saw an angel with thunderbolts and lightning who had been sent to the earth to bring God's justice upon mankind. The angel, "the executor of divine wrath," was about to strike the earth. Faustina begged for more time so the world could do penance, but to no effect. She then found herself before the throne of God. It was in the presence of the Trinity that she was given the means to extend God's mercy:

> The words with which I entreated God are these: "Eternal Father, I offer You the Body and Blood, Soul and Divinity of Your dearly beloved Son, Our Lord Jesus Christ for our sins and those of the whole world; for the sake of His sorrowful Passion, have mercy on us."
>
> As I was praying in this manner, I saw the Angel's helplessness: he could not carry out the just punishment which was rightly due for sins.[49]

The Lord's mercy has always been with us and available to us. Jesus was not giving Faustina a new doctrine, but a new emphasis on an essential aspect of His saving Gospel for this historical moment.

In Faustina's *Diary*, Jesus shows us how He extends His mercy to those who need it most, and how we are asked to participate with Him in doing this. As with all works of God, it is astounding:

> There are moments and there are mysteries of the divine mercy over which the heavens are astounded. Let our

---

[49] Ibid., nos. 474–475.

judgment of souls cease, for God's mercy upon them is extraordinary.[50]

The angels have been around since the beginning. They've seen the wondrous events in human history, including the creation of the world, countless miracles, the Incarnation, and Jesus' Resurrection. It would take something exceptional and perhaps unexpected to "astound" an angel, and yet Faustina tells us that "the heavens are astounded." Consider also Faustina's warning to us of "our judgment of souls." We should not be so proud as to make judgments about another's soul, even when all looks bleak. Who are we to put limits on God's mercy?

Faustina urges us in the midst of these spiritual battles never to accept defeat when it comes to the loss of a soul. "God's mercy sometimes touches the sinner at the last moment in a wondrous and mysterious way. Outwardly, it seems as if everything were lost, but it is not so."[51]

Dealing with the Devil

When we invoke God's mercy through the Divine Mercy Chaplet, Satan's plans can be thwarted. Souls destined for hell may be plucked from the devil's grip and rescued, even at the last moment. Faustina gives us an example:

Suddenly, I found myself in a strange cottage where an elderly man was dying amidst great torments. All about the bed was a multitude of demons and the family, who were crying. When I began to pray, the spirits of

---

[50] Ibid., no. 1684.
[51] Ibid., no. 1698.

darkness fled, with hissing and threats directed at me. The soul became calm and, filled with trust, rested in the Lord.[52]

The truth of God's mercy infuriates the devil. He hates all people, but especially those persons who successfully battle for souls by means of God's mercy. Jesus told Faustina that Satan "burns with a particular hatred for you, because you have snatched so many souls from his dominion."[53] In her battles, Faustina had several encounters with demons. They sometimes appeared as big black dogs ready to tear her to pieces. The demons taunted her, telling her that all her sufferings and sacrifices were useless. In their frustration over losing so many souls, they often complained, screeching and howling at her. She "saw that [her] suffering and prayer shackled Satan and snatched many souls from his clutches."[54]

Our entry onto the battlefield is through our current situations: the seemingly mundane things of everyday life. For Faustina, it was her life in the convent. Within the ordinary routines of consecrated life, Jesus commissioned her, "You are the secretary of My mercy. I have chosen you for that office in this life and the next life."[55] It seemed as though Jesus had assigned Faustina an impossible task, but He repeatedly assured her, "I will accomplish everything that is lacking in you."[56]

And Jesus did make up for what was "lacking in her" through others, beginning with her spiritual director, Blessed Father

[52] Ibid., no. 1798.
[53] Ibid., no. 412.
[54] Ibid., no. 1464–1465.
[55] Ibid., no. 1605.
[56] Ibid., no. 881.

Sopocko (1888–1975). By all appearances, there was nothing exceptional about Faustina's relationship with her spiritual director, but the two of them were about much more — they were both on a divine mission.

In 1938 Faustina died of tuberculosis; she was thirty-three years old. Propagation of the Divine Mercy message continued for sixty-two years, passing through times of severe testing and investigation as others brought Faustina's mission to its completion. On the Second Sunday of Easter in 2000, Pope John Paul II, who considered the Divine Mercy message to be his "special task,"[57] canonized Faustina Kowalska and inaugurated the first Divine Mercy Sunday.

Jesus' words to Faustina reveal to her, and to us, our identity as His knights on the stage of human history:

> I want you to become like a knight experienced in battle.... Let nothing drive you away from Me, not even your falls."[58]

> Know that you are now on a great stage where all heaven and earth are watching you. Fight like a knight.... Do not be unduly fearful, because you are not alone.[59]

We can know by faith, as Faustina did, that there is nothing mundane or common about our lives. Outwardly, there was nothing remarkable about Faustina; in fact, she (and those around her) were keenly aware of her shortcomings. But she knew who

---

[57] John Paul II, at the Shrine of Merciful Love, Collevalenza, Italy, November 22, 1981, The Divine Mercy, https://www.thedivinemercy.org/message/johnpaul/quotes.php.

[58] Saint Maria Faustina Kowalska, *Diary*, no. 1823.

[59] Ibid., 1760.

she was in Jesus Christ! Faustina understood the reality of the battle and its consequences, and she behaved accordingly, "I go through life in Your footsteps, invincible, with head held high, like a knight, feeble maid though I be."[60]

---

[60] Ibid., no. 1427.

6

The Power of the Eucharist:
Clare of Assisi

Clare of Assisi (1193–1254) embraced God's will for her life as the abbess of the cloister at San Damiano—she and her sisters were the female counterparts to Francis of Assisi's new mendicant order, the Franciscans. Clare and the nuns were veiled from the world in the enclosure of the monastery, where they sustained the work of the Franciscans through their hidden life of poverty and prayer.

Clare abandoned her noble status and worldly possessions in order to answer the Lord's call. This required a clandestine escape from her family home and her father, who had other plans for her life. Using the "door of the dead," which was reserved for removing caskets, young Clare slipped out of her home during the night. To her, this was symbolic: she had died to her former life and would now live a new life in total dependence on God.

Clare made her way through the darkness to the Portiuncula Chapel, where she met Francis and his brothers. As an act of detachment and in reception of her new life as a bride of Christ, Clare allowed Francis to cut off her beautiful blond hair. With her shorn head veiled and wearing a rough tunic, Clare was escorted by the Franciscan brothers to a Benedictine convent, where she could stay until suitable arrangements could be made for her and the other women who would surely follow.

The walls of the Benedictine convent did not prevent Clare's family from trying to rescue her. Her father, who had always made her decisions and intended to decide her future, could not understand why she would denounce her noble status to embrace the radical life of poverty offered by Francis. In the struggle to drag her from the convent, her veil was torn off, exposing her shorn head.

She pronounced boldly to her father, who was visibly shocked by her appearance, "The only spouse I will have is Christ, and further attempts to remove me from my chosen life will make me more steadfast!"[61] Defeated, he left.

Others followed Clare, including her sister Agnes. Young women gave up what were considered promising futures with the accompanying titles and lands to embrace a cloistered life of poverty and total dependence on God. The sisters were set up in a modest house across from the Church of San Damiano. When Clare was twenty-two, Francis appointed her superior, giving her his rule to live by.[62] The attraction to the Poor Clares, as they came to be called, continued to spread. During Clare's lifetime, similar convents were established all over Italy and parts of France and Germany.[63]

---

[61] Calamari and DiPasqua, *Ancient and Modern Saints*, 91.

[62] Father Joseph Vann, O.F.M., *Lives of Saints with Excerpts from Their Writings* (New York: John J. Crawley and Company, 1954), 260.

[63] Ibid.

Warrior Mother

Clare hoped for martyrdom and wanted to give her ultimate witness for her Lord in the Holy Land.[64] But martyrdom in the Holy Land was unrealistic for this virgin of Christ. But what if the opportunity for martyrdom came to her at the cloister of San Damiano? In 1240, the Saracens invaded Italy and were on their way to Assisi, where forty-seven-year-old Clare had been the abbess for almost twenty-five years.

The emperor Frederick II, in his ruthless expansion of territory, had been excommunicated by Pope Gregory IX, along with any man serving in his army. With no Christians willing to enlist, Frederick hired Saracens, Arab, and Muslim mercenaries. Villages were burned, and murders and atrocities were committed against the innocent and the defenseless. Monasteries were pillaged and destroyed, with unspeakable violations committed against nuns. Clare was sick in bed when word came that the Saracens were headed for San Damiano. There was no time to get help; the nuns were on their own. What is a mother to do when her daughters are in this kind of danger?

As ladders were being set to scale the walls of the convent, Clare, with assistance from her spiritual daughters, rose from her bed and went to our Lord, present Body, Blood, Soul, and Divinity in the Eucharist. In that desperate moment she prayed, "Does it please Thee, O God, to deliver into the hands of these beasts the defenseless children whom I have nourished with Thy love? I beseech Thee, good Lord, protect these whom now I am

---

[64] Bert Thoman, O.F.S., *St. Clare of Assisi: Light from the Cloister* (Charlotte, NC: TAN Books, 2017), 182, 231n176. She shared her desire with two of the sisters in the cloister of San Damiano who later testified to this fact.

not able to protect."[65] Her prayer was immediately answered, and she heard, "I will have them always in my care."[66]

In the church of San Damiano, Clare and her spiritual daughters prostrated themselves on the floor in adoration before the Blessed Sacrament. The Eucharistic Lord was their hope and their strength. Given the history of the Saracens at other convents, impending tortures and executions were feared. Come what may, the Lord of the universe was with them. He would have the final word.

When the Saracens burst into the church, they were caught off guard. On the floor lay the nuns in adoration. The sisters did not react to the intrusion; their full attention was on the Lord. The Saracens, with their foul reputation, always provoked a response. But not this time. None of the sisters were running to escape. No one was preparing to defend themselves or fight. Not one woman was screaming in terror. The mercenaries were then overcome with awe and fear and they fled.[67]

The Most Powerful Weapon of All

As we have seen demonstrated by Saint Clare of Assisi, spiritual weapons are confounding to the world but are powerful beyond space and time. Our Lord Himself offered His body on the Cross to defeat mankind's worst enemy—death. At Calvary, Satan was soundly and definitively defeated. Jesus' sacrifice is the greatest weapon against the devil.

We were not present at the Last Supper, the Crucifixion, or the Resurrection, but we are nonetheless invited to be there. God

---

65 Calamari and DiPasqua, *Ancient and Modern Saints*, 92.
66 Ibid.
67 Ibid.; Thoman, *St. Clare of Assisi*, 177–186.

is outside of time, and at Holy Mass we enter into His once-for-all sacrifice. We do not repeat it; rather, we participate in the Paschal Mystery. We are there.

During Mass, we are in the upper room at the Last Supper; we are at Calvary, the focal point of salvation history; we are peering into the empty tomb; and we are walking unknowingly with the hidden Jesus and the disciples on their way to Emmaus. Jesus said, "And behold, I am with you always, until the end of the age" (Matt. 28:20), and yet we know that He ascended to the Father, so how can this be? At Mass, our Lord is available to us in Holy Communion. We receive His Body, Blood, Soul, and Divinity, His presence, His "divine DNA." The Church teaches:

> There is no surer pledge or clearer sign of this great hope in the new heavens and new earth "in which righteousness dwells," than the Eucharist. Every time this mystery is celebrated, "the work of our redemption is carried on" (2 Pet. 3:13) and we "break the one bread that provides the medicine of immortality, the antidote for death, and the food that makes us live forever in Jesus Christ."[68]

Pope John Paul II wrote, "In reality Clare's whole life was a *eucharist* because, like Francis, from her cloister she raised up a continual 'thanksgiving' to God in her prayer, praise, supplication, intercession, weeping, offering and sacrifice."[69] This seems a counterintuitive means of waging war with the devil, but it is exactly how Clare, warrior woman that she was, trounced Satan.

---

[68] *Catechism of the Catholic Church* (CCC), no. 1405, quoting *Lumen Gentium* 3; St. Ignatius of Antioch, *Ad Eph.* 20, 2:SCh 10, 76.

[69] John Paul II, Letter for the eighth centenary of the birth of Saint Clare of Assisi (August 11, 1993), no. 7.

It is a mystery involving women, beginning with the ultimate warrior woman, the Blessed Mother.

Mary, *the woman* spoken of in Genesis, whose "seed" would crush the head of the serpent, participates profoundly in the plan of salvation, including the mystery of the Eucharist, "the antidote for death and the food that makes us live forever." The Body of Christ came from one woman, Mary; all His flesh, His entire humanity, came from His mother. The most powerful weapon against the infernal enemy of mankind came from a woman. The Blessed Virgin Mary is therefore caught up in the Eucharistic mystery:

> [There is] no body and Blood in Him except hers.... *"The Bread that I will give you is My flesh for the life of the world"* (John 6:51). Who gave that flesh? He was conceived of a woman. St Ambrose: "The Body that we consecrate comes from the Virgin."[70]

Because of Mary's fiat and through her maternity, we have the Eucharistic Jesus. The Christian who has just received Jesus in Holy Communion is therefore most feared by Satan and his demons. In a homily on the Eucharist, Saint John Chrysostom (349–407) makes this clear: "Let us then return from that table [having received the Body of Christ] like lions breathing fire, having become terrible to the devil."[71]

---

[70] Fulton Sheen, *Mary and the Institution of the Eucharist,* quoted in Peter J. Howard, *The Woman: The Mystery of Mary as Mediatrix in the Teaching of Fulton J. Sheen* (Phoenix: Leonine Publishers, 2014), 222.

[71] Saint John Chrysostom, Homily 46 on the Gospel of John, from *Nicene and Post-Nicene Fathers,* First Series, vol. 14, ed. Philip Schaff, trans. Charles Marriot (Buffalo, NY: Christian

The Eucharist is the defeat of the devil. Clare of Assisi understood this spiritual truth and testified to it with her life. Our participation in the Holy Sacrifice of the Mass and our reception of the Eucharist[72] opens heaven to us and renders Satan impotent.

Literature Publishing, 1889), rev. and ed. for New Advent by Kevin Knight, no. 3, http://www.newadvent.org/fathers/240146.htm.

[72] To receive the Eucharist, we must be in a state of grace, with no mortal sin on our soul.

Part 2

We Are Complementary in Mission

7

Mary and Joseph: God's Chosen Team

The Blessed Virgin Mary is all things to God: she is a daughter of faith to God the Father; she is the spouse of the Holy Spirit; and she is the Mother of Jesus. In that sense, we can accurately say in the words of the Council of Ephesus that she is the Mother of God. But even with her favored relationship with the Trinity, her obvious spiritual superiority, Mary needed Joseph.

There has never been a married couple in all of history with a more important mission than the Blessed Virgin Mary and her husband, Joseph of Nazareth. They had a child to raise, and this was no ordinary child. He was God incarnate. He was the Savior, the New Adam, the only One in human history who could restore mankind's relationship with God.

Jesus was at the center of Mary and Joseph's relationship. In this way, their marriage prefigures sacramental marriage in which Christ is central. Jesus was the motivation for everything they did, whether it was the ordinary tasks of life, or extraordinary events concerning Him. Mary and Joseph are the prototype for the ideal; they are the example given to us by God. And although they had different roles, the two were complementary in mission as the parents of the divine Child.

Jesus received His human nature completely from His Mother, the Blessed Virgin Mary. Even so, Joseph *is* the virginal father of Jesus[73] — not in the biological sense, to be sure, but in all the ways that make a man truly a father. Saint Luke writes of both Mary and Joseph as Jesus' "parents." And when Mary addresses her Son, she refers to Joseph as His father: "His mother said to him, 'Son, why have you done this to us? Your father and I have been looking for you with great anxiety'" (Luke 2:48).

The Divine Rescue Mission

At the proper time, the divine rescue mission was set in motion. Pride had caused the Fall of mankind. The restoration would come through its antidote — humility. And so, the promised Savior entered the world as a helpless, humble babe. And "the huge dragon, the ancient serpent, who is called the Devil and Satan, who deceived the whole world" (Rev. 12:9) sought to destroy the Divine Child:

> The dragon stood before the woman about to give birth, to devour her child when she gave birth. She gave birth to a son, a male child, destined to rule all the nations. (Rev. 12:4–5)

In early first-century Judea, this child would have been as vulnerable as any person could possibly be, as would His Mother. That's why God had given them a protector and a provider, someone faithful, faith-filled, fearless, self-sacrificing, and capable. That man was Joseph of Nazareth.

---

[73] Mark Miravalle, *Meet Your Spiritual Father: A Brief Introduction to St. Joseph* (Stockbridge, MA: Marian Press, 2015), chap. 6.

When King Herod sought to kill the child and ordered the massacre of the Holy Innocents, the evil king was outmaneuvered by Joseph. Joseph's faith, obedience, and prompt response to the life-threatening situation were powerful weapons against the enemy. When it came to the divine plan—that all-important mission to redeem the world—Joseph was all in, no matter what it meant, how it looked, or what sacrifices were required. Saint Matthew explains:

> When they [the Magi] had departed, behold, the angel of the Lord appeared to Joseph in a dream and said, "Rise, take the child and his mother, flee to Egypt, and stay there until I tell you. Herod is going to search for the child to destroy him." Joseph rose and took the child and his mother by night and departed for Egypt. He stayed there until the death of Herod, that what the Lord had said through the prophet might be fulfilled, "Out of Egypt I called my son." (Matt. 2:13–15)

During that night of terror, as the Holy Family prepared for their escape, one might imagine the Blessed Virgin questioning her husband: "Joseph, what's going on? Let's talk about this. I should have fifty percent of this decision." No, our Blessed Mother would never behave like that. She trusted God and His choice in Joseph as head of the Holy Family. Mary obediently followed Joseph's lead, and the family fled that night.

Shouldering the most important job on earth was probably not something Joseph had ever considered doing with his life, at least not until the angel came to him in a dream. But there he was, protecting the Incarnate Son of God, not simply from King Herod, a formidable adversary, to be sure, but also from Satan.

Joseph's fiat, his yes to God, was an irreplaceable component in the plan of salvation. Jesus and Mary were dependent on Saint Joseph's protection and provision. In this way, Joseph of Nazareth was the custodian of Christ's mission. His cooperation in the plan of salvation made Christ's redemptive work possible. We all owe Joseph our deep and sincere gratitude.

We Need Joseph, Too

Because of our relationship with Jesus, Joseph is also our spiritual father. In fact, the Church formally entrusted us to his paternal care and protection by declaring Saint Joseph "Patron of the Universal Church."[74] One of his many titles is "Terror of Demons," and rightly so. For Saint Joseph is a powerful ally in our battle against the devil, who has diabolical designs on our children, friends, and family.

Like Mary, we need Saint Joseph. Saint Teresa of Avila (1515–1582) had this to say about the efficacy of a relationship with the foster father of Jesus:

> I took for my advocate and lord [authority and father figure] the glorious St. Joseph and earnestly recommended myself to him. I saw clearly that as in this need so in other greater ones concerning honor and loss of soul, this father and lord of mine came to my rescue in better ways than I knew how to ask for. I only ask for the love of God those who do not believe me to try [or test] and they will see through experience the great good that comes from

---

[74] Miravalle, *Meet Your Spiritual Father*, 73, quoting Blessed Pius IX, *Quemadmodum Deus*, December 8, 1870.

recommending oneself to this glorious patriarch and being devoted to him.[75]

Mary was not disappointed in Joseph. She relied on him and was dependent on his protection and provision. Our elder sister in Christ, Saint Teresa of Avila, wasn't disappointed either, and neither will we be when we depend on him.

Complementary in Mission

In our current cultural setting, women are continually being tempted to pride, believing that they do not need men. If ever anyone had a claim to superiority, it would be the Blessed Virgin Mary, and yet she was dependent on Joseph. During the childhood of Jesus, God's cosmic plan of salvation was carried forward by this humble couple — together. God's design to vanquish evil requires both men and women, in friendships, in marriages, in families between brothers and sisters, fathers and daughters, and mothers and sons. We are in this struggle together, and we must not compete with one another over positions on the battlefield. If we quibble, argue, and get flustered over who does what, who is superior, whose job is more important, we will be distracted soldiers — a dangerous position that is easily manipulated by the evil one.

The Queen of Heaven and Earth humbly accepted her place as the wife of Joseph. Although their roles differed, with hers including obedience to Joseph, this couple perfectly complemented each other in the mission given to them by God.

[75] Teresa of Avila, *The Book of Her Life*, trans. Kieran Kavanaugh, O.C.D. and Otilio Rodriguez, O.C.D. (Indianapolis: Hackett Publishing, 2008), 28.

8

Together for Heaven: Zélie and Louis Martin

Zélie Guérin (1831-1877) was a spiritually committed young woman who had a heart for the sick and the poor. She believed she had a vocation to consecrated life. When her mother presented her to the Sisters of Charity of Saint Vincent de Paul, the mother superior dismissed the aspiring young woman outright, telling Zélie that she did not have a religious vocation. Her discernment process was over in a matter of minutes. This was indeed a disappointment for Zélie, and she mourned the loss of her hope in a religious vocation. Assuming her only option was marriage, she prayed that God would give her many children who would be consecrated to Him.

Zélie was mystical and intuitive, and she yielded her spirit to these aspects of her character. After entrusting her future to the Blessed Virgin Mary, Zélie interiorly heard, "See to the making of Point d'Alençon."[76] Believing that the directive to make the distinctive Alençon lace came from our Blessed Mother, Zélie obeyed without hesitation and entered the lace-making school.

---

[76] Fr. Stéphane-Joseph Piat, O.F.M., *A Family of Saints: The Martins of Lisieux—Saints Thérèse, Louis, and Zélie* (San Francisco: Ignatius Press, 2016), 49.

After learning the craft, which is quite intricate and can take years to learn, she set up her own business.

Louis Martin (1823–1894) hoped to join the hermitage of the Grand-Saint-Bernard in the Pennine Alps[77] and become an Augustinian monk. The remote, mountainous hermitage seemed to be a perfect fit for Louis. He was from a military background, preferred the outdoors and solitude, was intent on his spiritual welfare, and possessed an adventurous nature. He could see himself living out the rhythms of monastic life, but in this particular hermitage, also participating in courageous rescue missions, side by side with other monks, following their rescue dogs through the snow to find those who had been lost or covered by an avalanche. But it was not to be. Louis did not possess the necessary proficiency in Latin to enter. While he did begin his study of Latin, events unfolded that led him away from that pursuit. Louis became a master watchmaker with a business of his own. He was handsome, intelligent, devout, and, much to the disappointment of his mother, content with the single life.

One day, when they both happened to be crossing the Saint-Leonard Bridge, Zélie noticed the tall, handsome Louis. As she passed him, she once again heard an interior voice, "This is he whom I have prepared for you."[78] Less than three months later, on July 11, 1858, they were married.

If there ever were kindred spirits, it was this couple. They understood the other's desire for holiness and agreed to live as "brother and sister," refraining from the gift of marital relations for ten months until a wise priest counseled them otherwise. From their union, nine children were born. Two boys and one girl

---

[77] Ibid., 42.
[78] Ibid., 54.

died in infancy, and a little daughter, Hélène, died at the tender age of five. The remaining five daughters all became religious sisters. Léonie joined her aunt in the Visitation Convent. The other four, including the youngest, Saint Thérèse, entered the Carmelite Monastery of Lisieux.

Regrets and What-Ifs

I have a lot of trouble with this wretched Alençon lace which gives me the hardest time. I earn a little money, that's true, but, my God, it costs me so much!… It's at the price of my life because I believe that it's shortening my days, and, if God doesn't protect me in a special way, it seems to me that I'll not live long. I could easily be consoled by that if I didn't have any children to raise.[79]

What mother has not been frustrated like Zélie Martin and ranted (verbally or mentally) against the difficulties that must be endured to satisfy the demands of raising a family? Zélie, like many of us, was tempted by the "what-ifs" of her life. What if she (or we) had made different choices? When exasperated or heavily burdened, she was repeatedly tempted to regret that she did not live a different vocation. But Zélie refused the bait:

But quickly I tell myself, "I wouldn't have my four little girls, my charming little Joseph." … No. It's better that I struggle where I am and that they are here.[80]

Regrets can go deeper and be gut-wrenching. Zélie deeply desired to nurse her babies, and with each birth, she never lost

---

[79] Ibid., 112.
[80] Ibid.

hope of being able to do so. While awaiting the birth of Mélanie-Thérèse (another sister of our Thérèse), Zélie wrote about the situation in a letter to her sister-in-law:

> What troubles me is to think of having to put my baby with a wet nurse again. It's so difficult to find good people! I would also like to have the wet nurse live at our house, but that's impossible.... In the end, I think God will help me. He knows well that it's not laziness that keeps me from nursing my children because I'm not afraid of the effort.[81]

For a variety of reasons, it was simply impossible to have a wet nurse live close by or in the Martin home in Alençon, as Louis and Zélie would have preferred. With each child, there was much to consider concerning the selection of the wet nurse, and there was not always an abundance of good women from which to choose. Often the women had families of their own to take care of and therefore could not reside anywhere but in their own homes, which might be farther away than the Martins wanted.

After an intensive search, a nurse was hired in preparation for the birth of Mélanie-Thérèse. She lived on the rue de la Barre, not as close as the Martins had hoped. Despite the vetting that was done, it turned out she was an awful choice. The woman "disgracefully abused her confidence by letting the infant waste away."[82] Not wanting the child dying while still in her care, the wet nurse brought the child to the Martin home in the middle of the night. Zélie, seeing the condition and need of her baby, rushed Mélanie-Thérèse to another wet nurse some distance

[81] Ibid., 96.
[82] Ibid., 97.

from home. The desperate mother arrived with the starved infant only to find the woman sick in bed, unable to feed the baby. All options had been exhausted! What followed was two and a half hours of agony for both the mother and the child. Lying on Zélie's lap and drenched in her mother's tears, ten-month-old Mélanie-Thérèse died of starvation. If ever there was a temptation to self-recrimination, to live in regret, to harbor hatred for another, this was it.

An onslaught of emotions poured over Zélie. Her family was deeply concerned and "alarmed at this avalanche of troubles that might well destroy her health, which was already uncertain."[83] Zélie must have endured deep regret, much more so because the death had been preventable. *If only I had chosen or found a different wet nurse; if only I had gone to see the baby earlier; if only I could nurse my own babies; if only . . .* These thoughts must have haunted Zélie.

We can make decisions that are not evil in and of themselves, and even seem to be the right decision at the time, but still have devastating results. It may be due to immaturity or lack of knowledge, or a poorly developed conscience. We can make bad judgments and evil choices that we later come deeply to lament. Our regrets can sometimes be the poor decisions made and meted out to us and, regardless of our innocence, wound us deeply. In these situations, the battle against the enemy is in those regrets, tempting us to anger, bitterness, and condemnation of ourselves or others.

The devil is a creature, so he is not omniscient. He does not know the future; but he knows our past better than we do. The enemy speaks into our own minds, hoping we will accept his

---

[83] Ibid., 98.

thoughts as the truth. He cannot read our minds, even though it may appear as though he has. Because of their observation of all human history, the demons understand how to anticipate our actions and to tempt us most effectively.

Satan accuses us with what appears to be the truth. It may sound and feel like the truth. This is where we need to discern. If that "truth" makes us turn in on ourselves or distances us from God, then we know that it is not from God. Self-loathing is never from God, no matter what we have done.

Post-abortive women are often plagued with regret. It may be years later, but this wound against their womanly nature can manifest itself in a variety of ways: broken relationships—including relationships with family members and other children—health issues, emotional problems, and so forth. When circumstances line up such that a post-abortive woman finally comprehends the reality of what was done to her baby and to herself, the devil will try to imprison her in the "what-ifs," the anger against herself and those involved, and those gut-wrenching regrets. The devil becomes the accuser, tempting her to see herself through his twisted lens of self-loathing and accept it as the truth—but it's a lie.

On the other hand, our God, who *is* love, is omniscient. Our Lord *does* know such a woman better than she knows herself. He loves her and created her to be His daughter and live with Him eternally. His vision for her remains. The words the Lord spoke to Israel in exile through the prophet Jeremiah can be applied here: "A future full of hope" (Jer. 29:11).

Our Lord will not be outdone by evil—neither the evil done to us, the evil we do, or any combination thereof. When we repent, our deep regrets are transformed into a holy contrition full of hope, which can then be a springboard into greater holiness. God brings good from everything we give Him: our lives—past, present, and future—with all our mistakes and sins. Our weakness and our need for Jesus are a beautiful life-giving reality.

Winning the battle for souls starts with our own. Jesus, the Divine Physician, waits for us in the healing sacrament of Penance, where souls are released from Satan's grip. The would-be spoils of this war—our eternal souls—are rescued, one person at a time, in the confessional.

Jesus longs to heal our woundedness if only we will go to Him. Mother Teresa (1910–1997), an amazing warrior woman and saint, tells us how to win the battle when the evil one accuses us and wants us to deny Christ's vision for us:

> The devil may try to use the hurts of life, and sometimes our own mistakes—to make you feel it is impossible that Jesus really loves you, is really cleaving to you. This is a danger for all of us. And so sad, because it is completely opposite of what Jesus is really wanting, waiting to tell you. Not only that He loves you, but even more—He longs for you.... You don't have to be different for Jesus to love you. Only believe—you are precious to Him. Bring all you are suffering to His feet—only open your heart to be loved by Him as you are. He will do the rest.[84]

Zélie grieved the loss of all her children, but she endured a particular struggle with distinctive temptations when it came to the loss of Mélanie-Thérèse. Her family had been concerned with her emotional upheaval as she wrestled with her regrets concerning the child. But when her sister-in-law lost her newborn

---

[84] Father Michael E. Gaitley, M.I.C., *33 Days to Morning Glory: A Do-It-Yourself Retreat in Preparation for Marian Consecration* (Stockbridge, MA: Marian Press, 2012), 71.

son, Zélie reached out to the grieving mother with the fruit of her own struggles:

> When I closed the eyes of my dear little children and when I buried them, I felt great pain, but it was always with resignation. I didn't regret the sorrows and the problems that I had endured for them. Several people said to me, "It would be much better never to have had them." I can't bear that kind of talk. I don't think the sorrows and problems could be weighed against the eternal happiness of my children. So they weren't lost forever.... We'll see them again in Heaven.[85]

Real Family Life

In so many ways, the Martins were a typical family. They juggled the concerns of work, the education and health of the children, and the practicalities of managing an active home. And Louis and Zélie, despite their efforts, had in their little flock the proverbial black sheep. The parents worried over Léonie's developmental slowness and her teenage rebellion. But overall, family life was joyful. The family enjoyed outings together, and the girls put on plays for their parents. The liturgical seasons were observed with faithfulness, and the feast days fully anticipated and celebrated. They even had a dog named Tom.[86]

It was within the vocation of marriage that Louis and Zélie worked out their sanctification. They were on a mission in this world as married partners and good friends. While Zélie and

[85] Piat, A *Family of Saints*, 99.
[86] Ibid., 252. The dog, Tom, was brought to the family sometime after Zélie's death.

the girls were on a family trip to Lisieux, the couple exchanged letters. From Zélie to Louis we read:

> I'm with you in spirit all day, and I say to myself, "Now he must be doing such and such a thing." I'm longing to be near you, my dear Louis. I love you with all my heart, and I feel my affection so much more when you're not here with me. It would be impossible for me to live apart from you. I kiss you with all my love. The little girls want me to tell you that they're very happy to have come to Lisieux and they send you big hugs.[87]

Louis responded, addressing his wife as "friend":

> My dear Friend, ... it seems like a long time to me, and I'm longing to be with you. Needless to say, your letter made me very happy, except I see that you've tired yourself out far too much. So I strongly recommend calm and moderation, above all in your work.... I kiss you with all my heart, while waiting for the happiness of being with you again. I hope that Marie and Pauline are being very good! Your husband and true friend, who loves you for life.[88]

Radical Abandonment

At forty-one, Zélie Martin became pregnant with Thérèse. Zélie and Louis had lost four of their eight children, and Zélie was having health issues (four years later she would die of breast cancer). Another pregnancy in these circumstances was cause for others to question the couple's judgment. No one would have blamed

---

[87] Ibid., 159–160.
[88] Ibid., 160; letter dated October 8, 1863.

them if they had decided to abstain from marital intimacy, making what would appear to be a reasonable, prudent judgment. But if this holy couple had abstained (considering their first ten months of marriage, we know they had the strength of will to do it), the world would not have Saint Thérèse of Lisieux, Doctor of the Church, affectionately known as the Little Flower. Zélie anticipated the birth of Thérèse:

> It will be nothing but a pleasure to raise her. As for me, I'm crazy about children, I was born to have them, but it will soon be time for that to be over. I'll be forty-one years old the twenty-third of this month, old enough to be a grandmother.[89]

While pregnant with Thérèse, Zélie had a most amazing encounter with her unborn daughter:

> While I was carrying her, I noticed something that had never happened with my other children—when I sang, she would sing with me.... I'm confiding this to you [her mother-in-law]. No one would believe it.[90]

Zélie died of breast cancer when Thérèse was just four years old. But at her First Communion, Thérèse, in turn, experienced a beautiful encounter with her mother:

> How could my Mother's absence grieve me on my First Communion Day? As Heaven itself dwelt in my soul, in receiving a visit from Our Divine Lord I received one from my dear Mother too.[91]

---

[89] Ibid., 118.
[90] Ibid.
[91] St. Thérèse of Lisieux, *The Story of a Soul*, chap. 4.

Zélie referred to the time of pregnancy as the "advent" of the child to come. It was during the advent of Thérèse that the devil tried to uproot her peace. She was alone, thinking about certain warrior saints, who, because of their advanced holiness, were often badgered by the ancient enemy. But she assured herself, "Such outrages will not happen to me, only saints need fear them."[92] It was at this moment that she was physically grabbed by the shoulder and held by what felt like the claw of a large, powerful animal. Perhaps our Lord allowed this short harassment to demonstrate to her that she was on the path to sainthood. For a moment, Zélie was petrified; then she realized what was happening. This faith-filled warrior prayed with trust and continued in peace; the demon was not allowed to harass her further.

As our Mother Mary did, when Louis and Zélie Martin gave their fiat to the Lord, it was without reservation. Their radical abandonment to the will of God was a most effective strategy against the designs of the devil. The same spiritual principle applies to us. God does amazing things when we are in union with His will. There is simply no better place to be.

---

[92] Piat, *A Family of Saints*, 119.

9

If It Is God's Will:
Margaret Bosco and Her Son John

Margaret Bosco (1788–1856) could not have known that the lives of hundreds of homeless boys, a by-product of the industrial revolution, would be personally intertwined with her own. Margaret was poor, uneducated, and widowed. In her mind, the sort of influence she would have on these boys, whose benefits continue to this day, seemed beyond the realm of possibility. She was nearly sixty years old and finally experiencing a reprieve from her very challenging life when the Lord "uproot[ed] her from her house, her grandchildren and her serene daily routine."[93] She joined her son John Bosco (1815–1888) in Turin, Italy, where she mothered the needy boys he rescued off the streets. In this mission, her son was up against great evil—the devil's orchestrated destruction of many young souls. Preparation and training for combat on this battlefield had come through the trials and extreme challenges of their lives. John Bosco later wrote:

---

[93] Teresio Bosco, *Don Bosco: A New Biography*, trans. Silvano Borruso (Salesians of Don Bosco in the United States, 2003), 28, http://www.donboscowest.org/sites/default/files/resources/New-Biography-of-Don-Bosco_by-Teresio-Bosco_SDB.pdf.

I was not yet two when my father died. I do not remember his face. I only remember my mother's words: "You are now fatherless, Giuanin [Johnny]." As people streamed out of the room where my father's body lay, I stubbornly insisted on staying, "Come, Giuanin," my mother sweetly prodded me. [I answered], "If dad doesn't come, neither do I." "Come, son, your father is no more." With these words, that holy woman, sobbing, took me away, I cried as she did.... It is the first event of my life within memory.[94]

The early 1800s was a difficult time in Italian history, particularly for the farmers of the Piedmont region, which still suffered in the aftermath of the Napoleonic wars and was also in the grip of a drought. The people lived in extreme scarcity and famine. It was at this time and place that twenty-nine-year-old Margaret Bosco was widowed. She had three children to support. The oldest, nine-year-old Anthony, was a stepson from her deceased husband's first marriage. Margaret and Francesco had two sons together, Joseph and John.

The Boscos were farmers. The ease or hardness of life was directly correlated with the harvest, and during the worst of it, Margaret and her sons knew hunger. Regardless of her situation, Margaret had a job to do, assigned to her by Providence: to raise her boys to love God and seek His will above all else. This clarity of purpose motivated all her actions. From John Bosco we learn just how dire life was for this fatherless family:

A convenient arrangement was proposed to my mother. However, she repeated again and again, "God gave me a husband and God has taken him away. With his death,

---

[94] Ibid.

the Lord put three sons under my care. I would be a cruel mother to abandon them when they needed me most." On being told that her sons could be entrusted to a good guardian who would look after them well, she merely replied, "A guardian could only be their friend, but I am a mother to these sons of mine. All the gold in the world could never make me abandon them."[95]

Young John had a heart for God. At nine years old, he started having vivid, prophetic dreams, in which the Blessed Virgin was his guide. She showed him his future working with rough, unruly boys, turning them from wolves into lambs.

John felt the call to priesthood, which was almost inconceivable considering his situation. There was the farm — a necessity to the family's welfare, and there was the cost of an education, a financial impossibility. "If God wills it" was John's attitude. He lived in hope of becoming a priest.

The idea of an education for John grated on his brother Anthony, who was by now a young adult and managing the farm as the man of the family. John was almost twelve and getting old enough to contribute substantially to the workload, but whenever possible, he was found reading and studying. Anthony grew increasingly resentful. He had a sour disposition and was moody. John's physical safety was in question. John later wrote:

First to my mother, then my brother Joseph, Anthony peremptorily said: "Enough is enough. Stop all this grammar. I have grown up big and strong and never looked at those books." Afflicted and angry, I [John] said something

---

95 Saint John Bosco, *Don Bosco's Memoirs* (Bolton, UK: Don Bosco Publications, 2012), chap. 1, Kindle.

I shouldn't have: "Neither did our donkey go to school, and behold, he's bigger than you." At those words he flew into a rage and I just managed to run away from his beating. My mother felt most afflicted, and I cried.[96]

Margaret was a woman of prayer, and we can assume that she was often on her knees before the Lord. What should she do? She would not use her motherly authority to crush John beneath the expectation that he become a farmer. God had other plans for her youngest son. Yet she could not put Anthony out of the house, for the farm was his inheritance. Even if she could, she and her two younger sons could not manage the farm without him; it was their only means of support.

Within days, the situation at home escalated. John could not outrun Anthony, and he was beaten. Home had become a dangerous place for eleven-year-old John Bosco. Margaret was forced into making a heart-wrenching decision. She addressed her young son with the saddest words that would ever leave her lips: "Better if you leave home."

During planting and harvest times, it was common for boys to hire themselves out to farms; room and board was included in the arrangement. But it was February, and no such work existed. Moreover, John was considered rather young for hiring. Regardless, Margaret packed him a bundle of clothes, a couple of books, and a loaf of bread and sent him to seek employment at the area farms. It was a hopeful quest, one designed to secure John's safety. If he did not find work and a place to stay, John would be forced to return home. The day was ending, and no one had yet hired him when John arrived at the last house:

---

[96] Bosco, *Don Bosco*, 53.

Farmer Luigi Moglia looked at him in amazement. "I am looking for signor Luigi Moglia." "I am the one." "My mother sends me. She wants me to work for you as a stable boy." "But why does she send you out so young? Who's your Mum?" "Margaret Bosco, My brother Anthony ill-treats me, so she told me to look for employment as a stable boy." "My poor boy, this is winter. We hire stable boys towards the end of March. Be patient and go home." John felt disheartened and tired. He burst into tears of despair. "Take me, for charity's sake. Don't pay me, but don't send me home. Here"—he said with the strength of desperation—"I sit down here and stay put. Do what you want with me, but I stay put."[97]

John stayed at the Luigi farm for about two years.[98] People in his community noticed his sharp intellect and his budding holiness. Books were loaned to him, and he devoured them quickly. John taught himself, sometimes through painful trial and error, acrobatics and juggling on a tight rope. Keeping with a priestly desire to evangelize and save souls, John attracted young people by putting on shows. "You may not believe me, but by the time I was eleven I could juggle, somersault, do the swallow trick and walk on my hands, and even danced on the tightrope like a professional acrobat."[99] A typical entrance "fee" to his show was to first pray the Rosary or to listen to a word-for-word recitation of a sermon John had recently heard. He had a photographic memory.

We should not judge the younger version of Anthony too harshly. Consider his life. He had lost his biological mother at

---

[97] Ibid., 23–24.
[98] Ibid., 16.
[99] Ibid., 51.

a young age and then his father when he was nine. He was the oldest son by several years and had to shoulder the brunt of the farm labor. There was no safety net if the farm did not produce—destitution was always a couple of poor harvests away. When young John was getting old enough to help with the farm work but would rather go to school, study, and read, it greatly irritated Anthony. And there was his unpredictable and, at the time, volatile nature. Thankfully, we know that in later years there was no ill will and the family got along.

We could label John's early family life as "dysfunctional." But at the end of the story, we will see how God used this dysfunction to prepare a son and his mother to have an impact on the world for Christ. God is more powerful than the evil wrought in this fallen world. Saints come from families, even families with serious issues and problems.

John moved precariously along the unlikely road to priesthood, every step taken without the certainty that he would be able to continue. Although he and his mother did not live under the same roof, she was personally involved in his life and formation. During times of study, Margaret secured modest room and board for him, paying with sacks of grain. Through a series of events, and again with Margaret's influence, John was able to procure an education and then acceptance into the seminary. He later wrote about his conversation with his mother as he put on his cassock and prepared to leave:

> "My dear John, you have put on the priestly habit. I feel all the happiness that any mother could feel in her son's good fortune. Do remember this, however: it's not the habit that honors your state, but the practice of virtue. If you should ever begin to doubt your vocation, then—for

heaven's sake!—do not dishonor this habit. Put it aside immediately. I would much rather have a poor farmer for a son, than a priest who neglects his duties." ...

My mother was deeply moved as she finished these words, and I cried.

"Mother," I replied, "I thank you for all you have said and done for me. These words of yours will not prove vain; I will treasure them all my life."[100]

John studied for six more years, and in 1841 he was ordained a priest in Turin, Italy. His journey to this point had defied the odds. But Divine Providence, along with his mother, Margaret, had prepared this man for his particular impact on the world. John Bosco would battle the devil, going toe-to-toe, so to speak, with Satan for the souls of the street boys of Turin.

The devil's never-ending assault on the family is uniquely adapted to each era in human history. The family is under attack. It was during the industrial revolution, and it is today. The conditions are different, but the results are the same: without the protection of the family, members are vulnerable, easily wounded, and led astray, setting a trajectory of disintegration for future generations.

The industrial revolution, with its accompanying urbanization, was a terrible blight on the family. The unjust working conditions, thirteen- to sixteen-hour workdays for children as well as adults, the starvation wages, and the deplorable housing were all a part of its sad history. Many boys were without a future, without family, roaming the streets, living in hovels and vulnerable to many forms of exploitation.

[100] *Don Bosco's Memoirs*, chap. 18.

John Bosco understood these boys through his own experience: he had been fatherless, had experienced hunger, had endured the pain of separation from his family, and had known the desperation of begging for work and a place to stay. He also had an unshakable faith, which he credited to his mother. Could there be a more thorough preparation for a priest who is destined to minister to the impoverished boys roaming the city?

If the search for work proved futile, these unfortunate boys were pressured, often by hunger and desperation, into a life of crime. John Bosco began visiting the prison:

> I was horrified at the large number of 12- to 18-year-olds, all healthy and strong, intelligent looking, rotting there eaten by insects and starving for material and spiritual bread. I said to myself: *once out, these boys should find a friend to take care of them, helping, teaching, taking them to church on Sundays and holy days of obligation. They would not go back to prison.*[101]

And he resolved to be that friend.

In the effort to build trust with the incarcerated youth, John Bosco was dealt a lot of rejection, but he never gave up on them. One by one the boys began to trust him and attend his prison catechism: "As I made them conscious of their dignity, they felt a sense of goodness and resolved to improve."[102] John Bosco possessed a tender heart and he suffered because of it. Someone asked, "Why does that priest cry?" A youth answered, "Because he loves us."[103]

---

[101] Bosco, *Don Bosco*, 115–116.
[102] Ibid., 116.
[103] Ibid.

Receiving his directives from the Blessed Virgin in his dreams, he established oratories: centers for abandoned boys and juvenile ex-prisoners. These oratories offered recreation, education, and a safe place to belong. Here, John Bosco taught the boys their catechism lessons with patience and kindness. A man of action as well as his word, he took the time to interact and play with the boys, becoming their friend as well as their spiritual father. John Bosco loved his boys. They loved him in return and because of their affection called him "Don" Bosco, and the name stuck.

John would come to realize that he would need the help of a woman, and not just any woman. This dedicated priest needed a mother who had been through intensive spiritual-warfare training—someone experienced in battle with a proven faith. This partner had to be someone he could trust with his boys and who knew how to love as only a mother can. That person was his own mother, Margaret Bosco.

John asked:

Mother ... soon I will give hospitality to abandoned boys. You told me one day that if I became rich you would not set foot in my house. I am now poor and deep in debt, and ... live alone.... Would you be a mother to those boys?

Margaret realized the gravity of the request. It would mean giving up a life of relative ease with her family[104] and grandchildren to enter a life of endless work and poverty. John knew he was asking a great sacrifice of her. Ever faithful to the will of

---

[104] The troubles between Anthony and John had long been healed. John would visit his family on the farm and, in fact, convalesced there after a serious illness. Anthony had married and had a growing family. Margaret had been content living with them on the farm.

God, warrior mother Margaret Bosco did not hesitate to enter the battlefield on behalf of those boys. Feeling the weight of her fiat, she whispered, "If you think such a move is God's will, I'm ready to go right now."[105]

The pair walked together from the family home in Becchi to Turin (about fifty miles) and set up their residence. Before long, they had opened their home to orphans. "Mama Margaret" was often the first person the homeless boys met when they came knocking at the door. They would show up in the most pitiful state, always hungry, often cold, with nowhere to go and nearing despair. She would prepare something for them to eat, and they would tell her their heartbreaking stories. Was she reminded of her own life when she was forced to send her young son in search of work and a place to stay? She listened as one who understood their circumstances: *My mom died three nights ago; I am hungry; I was sent to the city to find work, but no one will hire me; I have no family left; If I return home, my dad will beat me.* When these destitute boys begged, "Don't send me away!"—and they always did—she would reply, "Don Bosco will never send you away."[106]

Mothering these boys would be challenging for anyone, and it was for Margaret. It required working from before sunrise until well after dark, and often dealing with serious situations that could not be put off until the next day. Margaret was feeling her age. She would have liked to return to her family in Becchi. But her fidelity to the mission kept her beside her son, caring for the temporal and spiritual needs of the boys whom the Lord had entrusted to them.

---

[105] Bosco, *Don Bosco*, 116.
[106] Ibid., 166.

Once, she almost reached a breaking point. The boys were playing war games and, in their exuberance, they had trampled her garden:

> The boys were asleep and she, as usual, was tackling a heap of clothes to mend.... Don Bosco was beside her, sewing patches.... She whispered: "John, I can't stand it any longer. Let me go back to Becchi. I work from morning till night, I'm a poor old woman, and those wild boys ruin everything. I can't go on like this."[107]

Don Bosco said nothing for a while. He caught her eye and then turned to look at the crucifix on the wall. She followed his lead and gazed up at the Suffering Servant hanging on the Cross. She then turned her attention back to the mending. Nothing more was said. Old and tired as she was, Mama Bosco would not abandon her post. She understood her mission in this war and would remain with her son John and "their" boys until her dying day.[108]

---

[107] Ibid., 176.

[108] Don Bosco founded the Salesians (named after Saint Francis de Sales) in 1854. With Saint Mary Mazzarello, he also founded the Daughters of Mary Help of Christians (the Salesian sisters) dedicated to the care of poor girls. Before Don Bosco's death, there were already more than seven hundred Salesian priests and brothers and as many Salesian sisters. Today there are more than forty thousand Salesian priests, brothers, and sisters throughout the world, carrying on the mission of Don Bosco. It is said that the Salesian Congregation was cradled on the knees of Mama Margaret.

10

Spiritual Friendship:
Jane de Chantal and Francis de Sales

Jane de Chantal (1572–1641), like Joan of Arc, was good on horseback. When she could, she sought solitude riding alone. She had much to consider, to ponder, and to pray about. Her beloved husband, Christopher, had been killed in a hunting accident, leaving behind twenty-nine-year-old Jane and their four young children.

She had been deeply in love with Christopher, embracing her life as the wife of a baron and as a mother. She managed the household and their estate, which included care for the poor, an expectation of the wealthy in late-sixteenth-century France. The baroness provided a soup kitchen at the back entrance of the castle as well as a rudimentary infirmary.

After months of intense mourning, Jane was not sure what to do. The cultural expectation for a woman of her young years and social status was remarriage. But in the months since Christopher's tragic, untimely death, she had changed. There was a stirring in her heart; a desire was growing within her. She longed to give herself completely to God. The young widow was not sure what to make of this, since she still had children to raise. But

Jane had made one firm decision: she would not remarry. Marriage was not necessary for her children's sake. They were heirs to her husband's holdings, their provision secure.

On one of her horseback rides, as she was returning to the castle from an infrequent, rarely used route, she saw a priest she did not recognize. He was walking out of the woods and did not see her. As she watched him, Jane heard an interior voice: "This is the man beloved of God and among men into whose hands you are to commit your conscience."[109] The thought brought her some comfort, but she was unsure, and so she continued to ride back to the castle. More than two years later, she would see this man again. Her father had invited the family to attend a Lenten mission. She and her children were seated in the front row when the new bishop of Geneva, Francis de Sales, began to preach.

When Francis saw Jane, he recognized her, but in a spiritual sense: "In the chapel of his home at Sales, it had been revealed to him that someday he might found a religious congregation."[110] The young widow before him would become the answer to that prayer.

After the talk, Francis inquired about Jane, and the two met. They both understood early on in their relationship that the Lord had connected them. Francis confirmed this in a letter he later wrote to Jane:

> It seems to me that God has given me to you. I feel more certain of it every day. I frequently entreat Our Lord to place us together in His Sacred wounds, and to give us the grace to give back there in the life we have received from

[109] Wendy Wright, *Francis de Sales and Jane de Chantal* (Boston: Pauline Books and Media, 2017), 34–35.
[110] Ibid., 42.

Him. I commend you to your good angel. Do the same for me, who am yours devotedly in Jesus Christ,

François, Bishop of Geneva[111]

After meeting a few times at family gatherings and going through a prayerful period of discernment, they entered into a formal arrangement; Francis would be Jane's spiritual director. Their relationship would grow and transform over the years from the spiritual direction of a father guiding his daughter, to include a deep level of friendship between spiritual equals.

After her children were set on their educational pursuits and their marriages arranged, Jane made solemn vows as a religious sister. She and Francis established the Congregation of the Visitation. It was a unique order for women with a religious vocation who, because of circumstances (age, health, or responsibilities), could not live cloistered or manage the stricter demands of most established religious orders. This was ideal for Jane, who, being a mother, never abandoned her children. Although she made solemn vows and lived as a religious, from time to time it was necessary to tend to the affairs of her children as they settled into adulthood.

When considering God's will for any new enterprise or action to be taken, at least three conditions must be satisfied:

1. Is there a need in the Church?
2. Is there the natural ability to do it?
3. Does the thought of it fill one with joy?

There is more to discernment, especially in weighty decisions, but the establishment of the Congregation of the Visitation met these three criteria, particularly with Jane as the foundress.

---

[111] Louise Stacpoole-Kenny, *St. Francis De Sales: A Biography of the Gentle Saint* (Rockford, IL: TAN Books, 2002), 139.

Because of Francis's arduous travel schedule, their friendship was primarily conducted through letters. Once or twice a year, however, Jane and Francis would have the opportunity to meet in person. Jane always came prepared with two lists: one regarding the rapid growth of the Visitation order, which continually required decisions and advice (before Jane's death, almost eighty Visitation monasteries would be established), and the other, her personal list. She longed to share with him her deepest thoughts:

> When I allow my heart to feel the incomparable joy of kneeling at your feet again as you give me your blessing, and I see this happening in my mind's eye, then I am suddenly overcome with sadness and the tears start, for I know I shall weep when, in God's mercy, I see you again. But I turn quickly away from the thought and don't allow myself to dwell on it. It is impossible for me to long for a meeting of set purpose; I leave everything that concerns me entirely to God and to you.[112]

At what was to be their last meeting in this world, Francis was pressed by his demanding travel schedule and insisted they discuss the needs of the congregation. Mother Chantal's personal list would have to wait. He promised to meet her at a later date when he would attend to all her personal concerns, giving them his priority. But it never happened. Two weeks later, Francis became ill and died unexpectedly. His death was a blow to Jane like no other she had experienced in life:

> Truly, I have never felt such an intense grief nor has my spirit ever received so heavy a blow. My sorrow is greater

---

[112] Wright, *Francis de Sales and Jane de Chantal*, 103.

than I could ever express, and it seems as though everything serves to increase my weariness and cause me to
regret.[113]

While a tomb was being prepared, Francis's body lay in state at
the Visitation Church. During this time, Jane planned a private
visit. There, alone, next to the body of her dear friend, she asked
him to make good on his promise as she poured out her soul. She
was consoled, knowing that from heaven, he heard her and was
tending to her spiritual direction as he had done so perfectly for
the last two decades. Mother Chantal was satisfied; Francis had
fulfilled his last promise to her.

Christian Friendship: A Tremendous Spiritual Weapon

Men and women need each other, and not just in married life, as
it was for Jane and her beloved late husband, Christopher. The
complementarity between man and woman exists not only in
the body but also in the soul. Jane's first "friend" was her father.
Of course, there was her marriage with Christopher, the beloved
husband of her youth.

Her brother, too, was a genuine friend. In fact, he arranged
the first meeting between her and Francis de Sales. And as Jane
journeyed toward religious life, he assisted her with her children,
seeing to the details of their education and marriage arrangements. They corresponded through the years, and the few letters
we have demonstrate a close bond between the siblings.

And of course, there was Francis, her spiritual director, who,
over time, came to be her closest friend on earth.

---

[113] From a letter she wrote to her brother, in ibid., 107–108.

Francis de Sales encouraged friendship and addressed it in his classic work *Introduction to the Devout Life*: "For those who live in the world … it is necessary to unite together in holy, sacred friendship."[114] Strict boundaries must be observed, however, if the friendship is to be efficacious: "Have no friendship, except for those that communicate with you the things of virtue."[115]

The sixteenth-century Spanish mystic Saint Teresa of Avila has given us good, practical advice regarding spiritual friendship. Looking back on her life, she realized that friendship would have been a great benefit to her: "It seems to me that if I should have had someone to talk all this over with, it would have helped me."[116] During her early years in the convent, this type of relationship was forbidden and thought to be a distraction that would compete with one's affection for God. Saint Teresa realized that true spiritual friendship is vital to the life of the Christian warrior. She goes as far as to tell us what "a great evil it is for a soul to be alone in the midst of so many dangers."[117]

The devil does not play fair; he hits us when we are down and exploits our vulnerabilities. Christian friends (both male and female) are a tremendous force against the manipulations of our evil enemy. The hunting accident resulting in the death of Jane's husband, Christopher, provides an example.

While Christopher and his hunting companion were crawling through the underbrush, stalking a deer, his companion's gun

---

[114] Fr. Joseph Esper, *Saintly Solutions to Life's Common Problems* (Manchester, NH: Sophia Institute Press, 2001), 28.

[115] Saint Francis de Sales, *Introduction to a Devout Life* (n.p.: Aeterna Press, 2015), chap. 19, Kindle.

[116] Teresa of Avila, *The Book of Her Life*, 40.

[117] Ibid.

accidentally discharged, mortally wounding the good baron. After a week of great suffering and Jane's ceaseless prayers and pleading for his healing, the beloved husband and father died. During his last days, Christopher forgave his friend for any carelessness that caused the accident. He put his affairs in order, adding to his will a clause stipulating that any relative who avenged his death would be disinherited.

Although Christopher was an example of Christian love in his last days, forgiving his hunting companion was not something Jane wanted to do. She had suffered a great loss. As a loving mother, she ached for her children, who would now grow up without their good father.

Jane was faced with a decision. Would she withhold or grant forgiveness?

In such situations, the battle against the enemy is in the tremendous temptation to nurture in our hearts bitterness and anger toward others. Spending our mental energies this way is risky, for it can cost us our souls. Jesus is clear about the necessity of forgiveness:

> If you forgive others their transgressions, your heavenly Father will forgive you. But if you do not forgive others, neither will your Father forgive your transgressions. (Matt. 6:14–15)

The phrase "not seeing the forest for the trees" is often true and demonstrates our need for our friends. When we are faced with pivotal situations in life, those who love us and want the best for us—that is, our Christian friends—can often see the things we miss and perceive the manipulations of the evil one. This is especially applicable when we are emotionally impacted, as we can see by the advice that Francis gives Jane:

All the repugnances of which you speak, all your feelings, aversions, difficulties, are all to my judgement for your greater good, and you are bound not to yield to them. You should keep making resolutions every day to fight and resist them.[118]

Francis was a good friend to Jane, and under his guidance, she was able to forgive her husband's friend and release the anger in her heart. It was, and usually is, a process. In that transformation, like most of us, she needed practical advice. Francis counseled Jane, telling her exactly how she should behave toward Christopher's hunting partner:

You needn't try to find a particular time or opportunity to seek him out; but if he should come to you himself, I would like you to greet him with a gentle, gracious, and compassionate heart. Doubtless it will be uneasy and agitated and your blood will boil, but what of it?[119]

The Armor of God, Battling the Devil, and Christian Friendship

In his Letter to the Ephesians, Saint Paul reminds all followers of Christ about the true nature of our struggle and the identity of our enemy. Therefore, he directs us to "put on the armor of God" (Eph. 6:11). The Roman soldier was the model from which he drew these spiritual analogies. In Paul's day, there was no better model to use. But what is not addressed, and on closer examination

---

[118] *Selected Letters of Saint Jane Frances de Chantal* (n.p.: Aeterna Press, 2105), chap. 13, Kindle.

[119] Wright, *Francis de Sales and Jane de Chantal*, 46.

appears to be a gaping vulnerability, points to a mighty spiritual weapon the Lord has given to us—Christian friendship:

> Finally, draw your strength from the Lord and from his mighty power. Put on the armor of God so that you may be able to stand firm against the tactics of the devil. For our struggle is not with flesh and blood but with the principalities, with the powers, with the world rulers of this present darkness, with the evil spirits in the heavens. Therefore, put on the armor of God, that you may be able to resist on the evil day and, having done everything, to hold your ground. So stand fast with your loins girded in truth, clothed with righteousness as a breastplate, and your feet shod in readiness for the gospel of peace. In all circumstances, hold faith as a shield, to quench all [the] flaming arrows of the evil one. And take the helmet of salvation and the sword of the Spirit, which is the word of God. With all prayer and supplication, pray at every opportunity in the Spirit. To that end, be watchful with all perseverance and supplication for all the holy ones. (Eph. 6:10–18)

In Saint Paul's assessment, there is no shield for the back of the soldier, and of course, the soldier cannot know what is coming from behind. It is in the formation of the troops, however, that we see how this all makes perfect sense. In a company of soldiers, those behind shield the backs of those in front. In battle, the Roman fighter had himself in mind, as well as the backs of his comrades in front of him.

What happens in this life determines our eternal destinies, but we do not go it alone. Jane de Chantal was not alone. The evil one tried to exploit her vulnerabilities, but she had a powerful ally in her friend Francis de Sales. It is the same for us. Like a company of well-trained Roman soldiers who move as a unified whole, we've got the backs of our brothers and sisters in Christ, and they've got ours. This is the power of Christian friendship.

Part 3

Mary, the Ultimate Warrior Woman:
Her Story and Ours

11

Our Story: The Truth and the Lie

Our story, the epic narrative of the human race, begins in the first chapters of Genesis. Here, religious realities are revealed using an ancient style, a kind of poetry with symbolism to convey profound theological truths. It is not a scientific explanation for creation and therefore might grate against our modern sensibilities. But if we set aside our narrow contemporary expectations, amazing, soul-impacting discoveries await us in the first three chapters of Genesis.

We are made in the image of God. His very breath endows us a with a soul, which animates us. We are created to live forever as embodied souls. Death—the separation of the body from the soul—came into the world as a result of sin and is unnatural for us.

"The LORD God then took the man and put him in the garden of Eden, to till it and keep it" (see Gen. 2:15). According to rabbinic tradition, the temple is the mirror of creation, and therefore Adam was considered a priest with priestly duties. To "keep" the garden can be understood as guarding the garden, as the priests guarded the sanctuary.[120] Eden is a holy sanctuary, and

---

[120] Scott Hahn and Curtis Mitch, *Ignatius Catholic Study Bible: Genesis* (San Francisco, Ignatius Press, 2010), 21, notes on Gen. 2:15.

Adam's job is to till and keep it—a work perfectly suited to him. Guarding the garden, however, implies that there is something to guard it from.[121] In fact, this enemy is revealed in chapter 3. The serpent in the third chapter of Genesis is identified in Revelation as the huge dragon, Satan (Rev. 12:3). The Hebrew word *Nahash*, which is used for "snake," is also "a draconic sea serpent that represents opposition to the Lord."[122] There was a dangerous enemy to keep out of the garden.

Eve entered into conversation with the devil, a fatal mistake. The devil tempted her with pride that she would be "like God." But she and her husband, Adam, were already like God, made in His image and likeness. The sad irony is that they were tricked into thinking that God was holding out on them, *that He couldn't be trusted.* "Man, tempted by the devil, let his trust in the Creator die in his heart" (CCC 397).

Where was Adam when the intruder was stalking his wife? The sacred author writes, "She took some of its fruit and ate it; and she also gave some to her husband, *who was with her,* and he ate it" (Gen. 3:6). The first man failed to guard the garden and protect his bride. Apparently, he stood there silently while the devil went after his beloved. He did not put his trust in God, and the results were devastating. "Death made its entrance into human history (cf. Rom. 5:12)" (CCC 400).

---

[121] "Behind the disobedient choice of our first parents lurks a seductive voice, opposed to God, which makes them fall into death out of envy. Scripture and the Church's Tradition see in this being a fallen angel, called 'Satan' or the 'devil' (cf John 8:44; Rev. 12:9)" (CCC 391).

[122] Hahn and Mitch, *Ignatius Catholic Study Bible*, 22, notes on Gen. 2:15; Job 26:13; Isa. 27:1; Amos 9:3.

Immediately after the Fall, the plan of salvation is implemented. God cursed the serpent, and, in the curse, we find His promise of redemption:

I will put enmity between you and the woman, and between your offspring and hers; They will strike at your head, while you strike at their heel. (Gen. 3:15)

Under Adam's failed leadership, humanity was banned from the Garden of Eden. That move may seem severe on God's part, but it was an act of mercy. Although, through disobedience, our first parents had eaten from the tree of the knowledge of good and evil, they had not yet eaten from the tree of life. Because of original sin, everything in creation was now perverted and disordered; death a reality. If our first parents had eaten the fruit of the tree of life, humanity would have been cursed forever in that fallen state.

The Lie Continues

The goal of the Christian is not emptiness with a peaceful absence of distractions, nor is it to be absorbed into an impersonal cosmic energy, a philosophy found in many Eastern religions. Rather, the Christian life is all about relationship; it is profoundly personal. We are in a process of transformation, becoming the persons that God created us to be in our fullest potential, without sin, beautiful, and with our unique personalities rightly ordered to perfection. We retain our personhood while we enter into the very life of the Trinity. Jesus is the Second Person of the Holy Trinity, and because of Him and our incorporation into the Mystical Body of Christ, we are brought into that reality. In this sense, we become divinized through this personal relationship with the Persons of the Trinity—not becoming another "god" but participating in God's very nature. This is the truth that Eve traded for a lie.

Saint Augustine famously wrote, "Our hearts are restless until they rest in you, O Lord."[123] Satan knows this yearning for God is built into every human heart by God, and the devil leverages it, baiting us to accept substitutes for God. Satan has been at this diversion as long as there have been souls to mislead. His lies never change; they are simply packaged differently to accommodate each age and culture.

Eve's fatal mistake is that she allowed trust to die in her heart. She was not receptive to all that God had in store for her. Rather, she grasped for what she thought was more.

Mary, the New Eve

In the first lines of the Gospel of John, the apostle draws an analogy to the creation story, using the language of Genesis. Only now John is telling the *re-creation* story:

> In the beginning was the Word, and the Word was with God, and the Word was God. He was in the beginning with God. All things came to be through him, and without him nothing came to be. (John 1:1–3)

In the re-creation story, there is a New Adam, Jesus Christ, and a New Eve, the Virgin Mary. Both play their respective roles in trust and obedience to the Father.

Eve was approached by the fallen angel Satan and chose to doubt God. Mary, the New Eve, was approached by the angel Gabriel and responded with total trust. Eve set a devastating

---

[123] Saint Augustine, *Confessions*, bk. 1, chap. 1.

trajectory for the human race, whereas Mary put into motion a correction that results in the redemption of fallen humanity.

Call to mind the promise given by God after the Fall: "I will put enmity between you and *the woman*, and between your off-spring and hers; They will strike at your head, while you strike at their heel" (Gen. 3:15). Mary is *the woman* spoken of by God.

At the wedding feast of Cana, Jesus addresses His mother as "Woman." He is identifying her as the woman from Genesis who participates in striking the head of the serpent.[124] Because of Mary's intercession for the wedding couple, Jesus begins His mission of redemption when He performs His first public miracle: changing water into wine. In this way we can see the promised rescue plan in Jesus. Creation is being remade in and through Him.

The Apostle John always refers to Mary as "Woman." We find this at the wedding at Cana (John 2:4), at the foot of the Cross (John 19:26), and when she is presented as the Ark of the New Covenant (Rev. 12:1). Saint John is making sure we understand that, just as Eve had a pivotal role in the fall of humanity, Mary also, as the New Eve, plays her part in reclaiming territory for Christ. Mary is *the woman* spoken of in Genesis who will bring forth the seed to crush the serpent. She is the warrior mother who goes to battle for her children.

Eve "was the mother of all the living" (Gen. 3:20). Mary, the Mother of Jesus, is also the Mother of the Church — meaning all the Church's members, her offspring, "those who keep God's commandments and bear witness to Jesus" (Rev. 12:17).

> In a very special way she [Mary] cooperated by her obe-dience, faith, hope and burning charity in the work of

---

[124] A reference to the Immaculate Conception of the Virgin Mary.

the Savior in restoring supernatural life to souls. For this reason, she is a mother to us in the order of grace.[125]

Some will continue to criticize the Catholic acknowledgment of Mary's participation in the plan of salvation. She is not our Savior—Jesus is. But God *did* involve her. Mary is essential to Christ's mission. She has her irreplaceable role as the New Eve in the re-creation story, in which our enemy is vanquished by our Warrior King, Jesus.

Jesus, the New Adam

Jesus Christ, the New Adam, handles His encounter with the serpent differently. During His forty days in the desert, when He is tempted by the devil, Jesus is obedient. He doesn't fall for the lie and the half-truths. He trusts the Father.

When all the powers of hell are thrown at Jesus during His Passion, He is not afraid of Satan's worst weapon, death. And He willingly sacrifices Himself for His Bride, the Church—something that Adam was not willing to do.

Because of Adam, we were removed from paradise: the tree of life banned from us, death our end. Jesus, the New Adam, crushes the ancient serpent. Death is defeated through the Cross of Christ—the Tree of Life. When we receive Holy Communion, we eat the fruit of this tree.[126] What was banned from humanity after the Fall is now offered in the Eucharist to all.

[125] Second Vatican Council, Dogmatic Constitution on the Church *Lumen Gentium* (November 21, 1964), no. 61.

[126] Mary gives us her Son Jesus. He is "the fruit of [her] womb." It is not an accident that Elizabeth refers to Mary's unborn child

There's no neutral position, no spectating. If we refuse to accept the reality of the ongoing battle with humanity's greatest adversary, we are already in the enemy's camp. If we are to take up our position in the campaign effectively, we must learn the devil's tactics and understand our own human weaknesses. We have our part to play; Jesus calls us to join Him in this great drama of human salvation. It's our story, and it continues:

> For a monumental struggle against the powers of darkness pervades the whole history of man. The battle was joined from the very origins of the world and will continue until the last day, as the Lord has attested.[127]

---

as "fruit": "Most blessed are you among women, and blessed is the fruit of your womb" (Luke 1:42).

[127] Second Vatican Council, Pastoral Constitution on the Church in the Modern World *Gaudium et Spes* (December 7, 1965), no. 37.

12

Old Testament Types for Our Mother:
The Ark of the Covenant,
Deborah and Jael, Judith, Esther

Throughout salvation history, God prepared His people for the coming of the Savior. The humblest, most colossal event in all the cosmos is the Incarnation, when Jesus was conceived in the womb of His Mother, Mary. God became man and dwelled among us (John 1:14). Nothing rocked our world more than God's taking on our human nature in order to redeem us. Time was split when He arrived, and a new era will begin when He comes again.

People and events in the Old Testament foreshadow the fulfillment to come in Christ. This is called "typology," and it helps us see the progression and realization of God's plan. For example, if we look at Moses through a typological lens, we see how he prefigured Jesus:

- When Moses was a baby, Pharaoh ordered the murder of all young Hebrew boys, but Moses was rescued (Exod. 1:22–2:10). Likewise, when Jesus was still under two years old, Herod gave a similar gruesome edict resulting in the slaughter of the Innocents, and Jesus, like Moses, escaped (Matt. 2:13–18).

- Moses instituted the Passover (Exod. 12); Jesus instituted the Eucharist at the Passover (Matt. 26:17–29).
- Moses saved his people from the slavery of Egypt (Exod. 1–18); Jesus saves His people from the slavery of sin.

These few examples demonstrate Moses as a type of Christ, and there are other types of Christ in the Old Testament. There are also "types" foreshadowing the Virgin Mary, her husband Joseph, the sacraments, and the Holy Catholic Church. Typology is evidence that the plan of salvation has been orchestrated by God throughout human history. Typology reveals the continuity of the divine plan.

In the typology of the Virgin Mary, we find Old Testament women who battled the enemies of God's chosen people. These loyal daughters of Israel often took great risks as they employed their wits, courage, and humility to take down Israel's enemies. Crushing the head of the serpent is a recurring theme with the Old Testament warrior types.[128] Theirs, however, was a temporal battle prefiguring the Virgin Mary, the New Eve, who engages in a war for the eternal souls of her children, "the rest of her offspring" (Rev. 12:17).

Old Testament types foreshadowing a fulfillment in God's plan of salvation are not limited to persons. The Ark of the Covenant is also a type prefiguring the Blessed Virgin Mary. If we are to be victorious over our greatest enemy, Satan, we need our Heavenly Mother to lead the way as indicated by her title, Ark of the New Covenant.

---

[128] There are other types for the Virgin Mary that are found in the Old Testament—not only the warrior types included in this book.

The Ark of the Covenant

The Ark of the Covenant was the chest containing the tables of the law given to Moses and was kept in the holy of holies of the tabernacle. When its construction had been completed, the glory cloud of the Lord filled the tabernacle, covering the ark.[129] The glory cloud, or *Shekinah*, indicated God's intimate presence with His people. But let's be very clear: the ark was not worshipped. Rather, the ark allowed the people to draw near to God. We find a similar "covering" in the angel Gabriel's answer to Mary concerning the conception of Jesus: "The Holy Spirit will come upon you, and the power of the Most High will overshadow [cover] you. Therefore, the child to be born will be called holy, the Son of God" (Luke 1:35). It is through the Ark of the *New* Covenant, Mary, that God becomes one of us and dwells intimately with us. Because of Mary, we not only draw near to God, but He shares our human nature, and we therefore are allowed to share in His divinity.

The Ark contained three sacred items (Heb. 9:4), each of which corresponds to the Blessed Virgin Mary:

- A gold jar contained the manna from heaven; Mary enfleshed in her womb, the true bread from heaven, Jesus Christ.
- The staff of Aaron that had sprouted, representing the true priesthood (Num. 17:16–23); our Lord Jesus Christ is the eternal High Priest, who received His humanity in the womb of Mary.
- The stone tablets of the old covenant, which Moses received on Mount Sinai; Jesus Christ is the New and

[129] "Then the cloud covered the tent of meeting, and the glory of the LORD filled the tabernacle (Exod. 40:34).

Eternal Covenant and was made present to us through Mary, His mother.

In his Gospel, Luke reveals stunning correspondences between the ark during the reign of King David[130] and the Virgin Mary. The Jews in the apostolic age reading the Gospel of Luke would have recognized this parallelism.

• King David sets out for the hill country of Judah, and so does Mary (2 Sam. 6:2; Luke 1:39).

• King David's response to the presence of the Ark mirrors Elizabeth's response when Mary arrives (2 Sam. 6:9; Luke 1:43).

• David (with the Ark) and Mary both stay three months, and the household is blessed by it (2 Sam. 6:11; Luke 1:56).

• David and the unborn John the Baptist are both prompted to dance and leap (2 Sam. 6:14; Luke 1:41).

• Elizabeth "cried out in a loud voice" (Luke 1:42), which mirrors the Levitical priests' shouts of praise before the presence of God contained in Ark of the Covenant (see 2 Sam 6:15). Elizabeth is a descendant of Aaron,[131] for she comes from the Levitical priestly family and lifts her voice before Mary, addressing her as "the mother of my Lord."

When Jerusalem fell to the Babylonians in 586 B.C., the Ark was hidden by Jeremiah, who prophesied, "The place is to remain unknown until God gathers his people together again and shows them mercy" (2 Macc. 2:7). The recovery of the Ark, for the

---

[130] Specifically referring to chapter 6 of 2 Samuel.

[131] Scott Hahn, ed., *Catholic Bible Dictionary* (New York: Doubleday, 2009), 242–243.

Jewish people, was central to their hopes for the Messiah and the reestablishment of the Davidic Kingdom. The Apostle John knew this. In the book of Revelation, he builds the narrative to the climatic point and presents to the reader the long-awaited Ark of the Covenant. Only this time, it is not the foreshadowing type but the Ark of the New Covenant:

> Then God's temple in heaven was opened, and the ark of his covenant could be seen in the temple. There were flashes of lightning, rumblings, and peals of thunder, an earthquake, and a violent hailstorm.[132] A great sign appeared in the sky, a woman clothed with the sun, with the moon under her feet, and on her head a crown of twelve stars. She was with child. (Rev. 11:19–12:2)

Mary, the Ark of the New Covenant

The children of Israel brought the Ark with them into battle precisely because it ensured God's presence;[133] it was a sacred instrument of Holy War. At the Lord's instructions, the ark occupied the most prominent position at the Battle of Jericho (Josh. 6:8–9). Victorious at Jericho, the Ark was carried by the priests at the front of the procession when Joshua led Israel into the Promised Land.[134]

---

[132] The Scriptures were not originally divided into chapters. Immediately following this verse at the beginning of the next chapter we read a description of the "ark" of His (the Lamb's) covenant.

[133] "They are to make a sanctuary for me, that I may dwell in their midst" (Exod. 25:8).

[134] Joshua is a type for Jesus, who will lead His people to heaven, and the real Promised Land is eternal life in heaven.

As Jesus leads us into the Promised Land of Heaven, the Virgin Mary, as the Ark of the New Covenant, plays a central role in the battle against the devil. Like the children of Israel who needed the Ark with them if they were to be victorious in battle, we need Our Lady with us if we hope to defeat the devil "who prowls throughout the world seeking the ruin of souls."[135]

Deborah and Jael

In the fourth chapter of the book of Judges, we find another type for the Blessed Virgin Mary, Deborah. She was a wife, prophetess, and judge of Israel during a twenty-year period of oppression under the Canaanites. The cruel commander of the Canaanite army was a man named Sisera.

Deborah summoned a Hebrew man, Barak from Kedesh, and delivered the Lord's message to him. He would lead an army against the Canaanites, and the Lord would deliver the enemy into his hands. But Barak was afraid; his obedience was conditional. He answered Deborah: "If you come with me, I will go; if you do not come with me, I will not go" (Judg. 4:8).

Deborah believed the Lord, who had told her, "I will draw out Sisera, the general of Jabin's army ... and I will give him into your hands" (see Judg. 4:7), and she replied without hesitation, "I will certainly go with you, but you will not gain glory for the expedition on which you are setting out, for it is into a woman's power that the LORD is going to sell Sisera" (Judg. 4:9).

It is significant that Israel's commander wanted Deborah to go with him, and that she went without hesitation. Is it any different when we go into battle for the souls of our children,

---

[135] From the prayer to Saint Michael the Archangel.

our friends, and our families and ask our Lady to lead the way? Deborah prefigures Mary in many ways. She hears God, shows others the way the Lord wants them to go, leads the attack against the enemy, and does not hesitate in her obedient responses to the Lord's will.

The narrative progressed as the Lord had foretold: "The entire army of Sisera fell beneath the sword, not even one man surviving" (Judg. 4:16). But Sisera escaped on foot to the tent of Jael, who was a Kenite and thought to be a Canaanite ally. She welcomed the commander, gave him milk, and covered him with a rug to hide him. Sisera, who must have been exhausted, relaxed under Jael's care, and fell asleep.

Like other warrior women in the Old Testament, and reminiscent of "crushing the head of the serpent" from Genesis, Jael went for the head of the enemy of Israel:

> Jael, wife of Heber, got a tent peg and took a mallet in her hand. When Sisera was in a deep sleep from exhaustion, she approached him stealthily and drove the peg through his temple and down into the ground, and he died. (Judg. 4:21)

Thus, Israel's freedom was gained by the obedience, courage, and strength of two women: Deborah and Jael.

Judith

Imagine an opponent who is so powerful and influential that the known world considers him a god? This is what we find in the story of Judith. Cities were conquered as the Assyrian forces of King Nebuchadnezzar advanced, plundering, killing, enslaving, and destroying all in their path.

When an adviser attempted to enlighten Holofernes, the ranking general of Nebuchadnezzar's army, by recounting Israel's history and the might of their God, Holofernes was enraged. In his pride and arrogance, he pronounced, "Who is God beside Nebuchadnezzar? He will send his force and destroy them from the face of the earth. Their God will not save them.... Their mountains shall be drunk with their blood, and their plains filled with their corpses" (Jdt. 6:2–4).

The campaign against Israel began at the town of Bethulia, the home of a devout widow, Judith. In an effort to wear the people down by thirst, the Assyrians cut off the water supply to the city. In due time, they planned to move in with little or no resistance. The entire Assyrian army, with its infantry, chariots, and cavalry surrounded the city and encamped there for over a month as they waited for the reservoirs and cisterns of Bethulia to run dry.

The people were desperate and begged the high priest Uzziah and the leaders of the city to negotiate with Holofernes. They would rather be enslaved than be annihilated. Uzziah encouraged the people to wait five more days before surrendering; it is during this time that Judith entered the story.

Judith was a pious, faithful Israelite widow. She was wealthy, beautiful, and highly regarded by her people: "No one had a bad word to say about her, for she feared God greatly" (Jdt. 8:8). She was also known for her wisdom.[136] For Judith, the situation was a blessing, a test for which they should thank God![137] This wise

---

[136] "For today is not the first time your wisdom has been evident, but from your earliest days all the people have recognized your understanding, for your heart's disposition is right" (Jdt. 8:29).

[137] "Besides all this, let us give thanks to the Lord our God for putting us to the test as he did our ancestors. Recall how he dealt with Abraham, and how he tested Isaac" (Jdt. 8:25–26).

widow of Israel was not fearful; rather, she saw an opportunity to inspire and fortify the rest of Judea. She encouraged Uzziah and the city leaders, "Let us set an example for our kindred. Their lives depend on us, and the defense of the sanctuary, the temple and the altar" (Jdt. 8:24).

Judith prayed intently and, with the help of the Lord, came up with a plan. She addressed the high priest and the city leaders:

> "Listen to me! I will perform a deed that will go down from generation to generation among our descendants. Stand at the city gate tonight to let me pass through with my maid; and within the days you have specified before you will surrender the city to our enemies, the Lord will deliver Israel by my hand. You must not inquire into the affair, for I will not tell you what I am doing until it has been accomplished." Uzziah and the city leaders said to her, "Go in peace, and may the Lord God go before you to take vengeance upon our enemies!" (Jdt. 8:32–35)

Judith and her maid left the city gate and approached the Assyrians. The guards were stunned by her beauty and courage and took her to their commander. Holofernes was also beguiled by Judith and compelled her to dine with him. But she insisted that she must eat the prescribed food of her people. Therefore, she and her maid were allowed to bring a basket of food with them. Through repeated visits, the guards become accustomed to Judith and her maid coming with a large basket and going out at night to pray. Meanwhile, Holofernes has been waiting for the moment when he would seduce Judith but she turned his scheme back on him:

> So she proceeded to put on her festive garments and all her finery.... Then Judith came in and reclined. The heart

of Holofernes was in rapture over her and his passion was aroused. He was burning with the desire to possess her, for he had been biding his time to seduce her from the day he saw her.... Holofernes, charmed by her, drank a great quantity of wine, more than he had ever drunk on any day since he was born. (Jdt. 12:15–16, 20)

Knowing Holofernes's plan to seduce Judith, his men left the couple alone. Judith encouraged the deluded Holofernes to drink wine with abandon, and the mighty Assyrian commander passed out. Judith saw before her the great enemy of her people, sprawled out upon the bed. The Lord had delivered him into her hands. She prayed, "Strengthen me this day, Lord, God of Israel!" (Jdt. 13:7). Judith grasped her enemy's own sword in one hand and his hair in her other hand, and she cut his head off with two mighty blows.

The bloody head of Holofernes was given to her maid and put into their food bag, which had become a usual sight among the Assyrian guards. With the Assyrian commander's head hidden in the food bag, Judith and her maid left that night; "the two went out together for prayer as they were accustomed to do" (Jdt. 13:10).

With the head of their enemy delivered to them, the Israelites advanced on the Assyrian army. And when the guards rushed to waken their commander, they found the headless body of Holofernes and cried out, "The slaves have duped us! One Hebrew woman has brought shame on the house of King Nebuchadnezzar. Look! Holofernes on the ground—without a head!" (Jdt. 14:18). They broke rank and were scattered; the enemy was defeated.

The book of Judith was most likely written during the Maccabean Revolt (160–167 B.C.). At this time in Jewish history, an epic story like this certainly would serve to inspire God's people. The story emphasizes faithfulness, trust, courage, and the Lord's protection. This book is included in the Catholic canon of Sacred Scripture, coming from the Septuagint — the Old Testament Greek Scriptures, which Jesus Himself studied and quoted.[138]

When looking at the book of Judith, we can recognize a foreshadowing of the Virgin Mary. There are many similar pronouncements by Judith and Mary. For example, Judith prophesized about herself, "Listen to me! I will perform a deed that will go down from generation to generation among our descendants" (Jdt. 8:32). And Mary said, "My soul proclaims the greatness of the Lord; my spirit rejoices in God my savior. For he has looked upon his handmaid's lowliness; behold, from now on will all ages call me blessed" (Luke 1:46–48).

Judith is a type of Mary. She is an obedient, trusting, courageous, faithful daughter of Israel who fights the enemy of her people. Going for the head of her adversary, Judith decapitates Holofernes. In turn, Mary, as the New Eve and the Mother of the Messiah, fulfills her unique role in salvation history by participating with her Son Jesus in crushing the head of the serpent.

Queen Esther

During the reign of King Ahasuerus (the Hebrew name for Xerxes I of Persia),[139] Mordecai, a Jew in exile, along with his niece Esther,[140] lived in Susa, the capital city of Persia. Esther was lovely,

---

[138] The earliest Greek translation of the Old Testament from the original Hebrew, used in the time of Christ.

[139] Most likely between 486 and 465 B.C.

[140] Esther was an orphan, and Mordecai adopted her as his own daughter (Esther 2:7).

and through a series of events (we might think of a beauty contest), King Ahasuerus chose Esther to be his new queen. Contending for the queenship of Persia was not in Esther's heart, but she participated, keeping secret her Jewish identity in obedience to her uncle Mordecai. We can see from her prayer to the "God of Abraham, God of Isaac, and God of Jacob" that Esther was a Jewish woman who distained the opulence afforded her as a Gentile queen:

> You [Lord] know all things. You know that I hate the pomp of the lawless, and abhor the bed of the uncircumcised or of any foreigner. You know that I am under constraint, that I abhor the sign of grandeur that rests on my head [the crown] when I appear in public. I abhor it like a polluted rag, and do not wear it in private. (Esther 4, supplemental chapter C:26–27)[141]

Mordecai discovered a plot contrived by the king's chief adviser, Haman, to annihilate all the Jews living in Persia. He therefore appealed to his niece, Queen Esther, indicating that she was in her position for a reason: "Perhaps it was for a time like this that you became queen?" (Esther 4:14).

The penalty for coming into the presence of the king without a summons was death. With the date set for the extermination of her people quickly approaching, Esther did not have the leisure of waiting for her next summons. Despite the risk, she would need to go to the king.

To prepare for her uninvited audience with the king, she and all her people would fast and pray for three days. She told her

---

[141] From the additional chapters in Esther which were written after the Hebrew text and are found in the Greek Septuagint Old Testament.

uncle Mordecai, "Thus prepared, I will go to the king, contrary to the law. If I perish, I perish!" (Esther 4:16).

Esther, her maids, Mordecai, and all the Jewish people fasted and prayed in preparation for Esther's appearance before the king. "On the third day, ending her prayers, she took off her prayer garments and arrayed herself in her splendid attire" (Esther 4, supplemental chapter D:1). Esther walked into the courtyard of the king. When King Ahasuerus saw her there, he extended his scepter; she had won his favor. Curious and impressed with her courage, he asked her to reveal her request, offering up to half his kingdom. She asked only that he and his chief adviser, Haman (the one responsible for the plot to kill the Jews), come and dine at a banquet she would prepare. The king was intrigued, and he accepted her invitation for himself and for his chief adviser.

While drinking wine at her banquet, King Ahasuerus again put the question to her, "Whatever you ask, Queen Esther, shall be granted you. Whatever request you make, even for half the kingdom, shall be honored" (Esther 7:2). She then revealed her Jewish identity and the reason she had risked her life to speak to the king:

> If I have found favor with you, O king, and if it pleases your majesty, I ask that my life be spared, and I beg that you spare the lives of my people. For we have been sold, I and my people, to be destroyed, killed, and annihilated. (Esther 7:3–4)

Queen Esther continued her explanation and revealed Haman's evil plot to commit genocide against her people. Haman's plot was foiled and turned against him. The execution he had personally planned for Mordecai became his own death sentence:

"Haman [was] impaled on the stake he had set up for Mordecai" (see Esther 7:9–10).

Queen Esther is another Old Testament woman who pre-figured Mary. Esther is lowly, but because of her beauty, she is chosen to be queen. Mary, too, is lowly, but because of the beauty of her soul, she is chosen to be the Mother of Jesus and, after her Assumption, is crowned queen. Esther sacrificed and prayed for her people; she went before the king to intercede on their behalf, and she was heard. Mary sacrificed a great deal for our salvation. Our Blessed Mother and Queen goes to King Jesus on our behalf; it is through Jesus that our enemy is vanquished.

Queen Esther saved her people. Her strategy included obedience, communal prayer and fasting, humbling herself before the Lord, and utilizing her unique position as queen. Her uncle Mordecai was correct when he suggested to Esther that "perhaps it was for a time like this that you became queen." Considering our unique situation, we can ask a similar question: "Perhaps it is for a time like this that I live in these particular circumstances."

13

The Heart of the Matter:
Our Blessed Mother Mary

"I am the Lady of the Rosary."[142] These are the words of the Blessed Virgin Mary when she revealed her identity to three children of Fatima, Portugal, in 1917. She taught them, "Pray, pray very much, and make sacrifices for sinners; for many souls go to hell, because there are none to sacrifice themselves and to pray for them."[143]

In her apparitions, Our Lady was giving the three young visionaries personal spiritual-warfare training and equipping them with a mighty weapon, the Rosary. The Queen Mother herself commissioned these young ones into Christ's mission for the salvation of souls. By virtue of our Baptism, we too have been commissioned into the same mission.

The visionaries at Fatima were nine-year-old Lúcia dos Santos and her cousins (brother and sister) eight-year-old

---

[142] Fr. Andrew Apostoli, *Fatima for Today* (San Francisco: Ignatius Press, 2010), 123.

[143] Ibid., 167; Lucia dos Santos, *Fatima in Lucia's Own Words: Sister Lucia's Memoirs*, ed. Fr. Louis Kondor, trans. Dominican Nuns of Perpetual Rosary (Fatima: Postulation Centre, 1976), 24.

Francisco and seven-year-old Jacinta Marto. These illiterate peasant children were heaven's choice; the Mother of God came to them with messages for the entire world. Saint Paul famously wrote, "God chose the foolish of the world to shame the wise, and God chose the weak of the world to shame the strong" (1 Cor. 1:27).

The soul-saving message of Fatima—to pray the Rosary, to make reparation for sinners, and to promote the consecration to the Immaculate Heart of Mary—is still relevant today, perhaps even more so. And Mother Mary did not spare the truth when she trained her young warriors for battle. Rather, she showed them hell, where poor sinners go:

> We saw as it were a sea of fire. Plunged in this fire were demons and souls in human form, like transparent burning embers, all blackened or burnished bronze, floating about in the conflagration ... amid shrieks and groans of pain and despair, which horrified us and made us tremble with fear.[144]

Within three years of the apparitions, Mary had gathered up two of her little saints. Francisco and Jacinta died during an influenza epidemic. Both willingly suffered for the salvation of sinners, and both, knowing they would die young, sincerely looked forward to heaven.[145]

In a vision to Jacinta, Mary offered to take her to heaven, but the little girl made a heroic sacrifice and chose to remain on earth a little longer in order to suffer to make reparation for

---

[144] Apostoli, *Fatima for Today*, 60.
[145] On May 13, 2017, the hundredth anniversary of the first apparition, Francisco and Jacinta were canonized by Pope Francis.

sinners. Up to this point, little Jacinta had proved she could endure a variety of very difficult hardships. The worst for her, however, was yet to come. Loneliness was her greatest suffering, and at nine years old, she died alone in a hospital, far from her family and friends.

Sister Lúcia was called to religious life and lived until she was ninety-seven. She points to the Rosary as a weapon that the Virgin Mary has spiritually fortified and strengthened for the needs of our times:

> The Most Holy Virgin, in these last times in which we live, has given a new efficacy to the recitation of the rosary to such an extent that there is no problem, no matter how difficult it is, whether temporal or above all spiritual, in the personal life of each one of us, of our families ... that cannot be solved by the rosary. There is no problem, I tell you, no matter how difficult it is, that we cannot resolve by the prayer of the holy rosary.[146]

When praying and meditating on the mysteries of the Rosary, we accompany Mary and Jesus as they work out our salvation. We travel with them from the Incarnation through Jesus' ministry all the way to the Cross. We experience the Resurrection on the first Easter morning and accompany the early Church up to the crowning of the Queen of Heaven. We see that the devil is crushed, and mankind's worst enemy, death, is vanquished. The Rosary is a formidable spiritual weapon. Like many holy men and women, Mother Teresa understood the power of the

---

[146] Quoted in Donald H. Calloway, M.I.C., *Champions of the Rosary: The History and Heroes of a Spiritual Weapon* (Stockbridge, MA: Marian Press, 2016), 247.

Rosary. When in an airport, travelers were asked if they carried any weapons. Mother Teresa complying with the request of the security officer held out her weapon: her rosary.[147]

At the Heart of the Matter

Father Michael Gaitley writes, "The heart refers to one's inner life and the seat of the indwelling Holy Spirit."[148] The heart is the essence of the person. It is at the core of our identity; it involves our thinking, our will, our love, and our decisions.

Through the Immaculate Heart of the Virgin Mary, souls are rescued, graces procured, and the plans of the devil intercepted. Our Blessed Mother explained this to the children of Fatima:

> You have seen hell where the souls of poor sinners go. To save them, God wishes to establish in the world devotion to my Immaculate Heart. If what I say to you is done, many souls will be saved and there will be peace.[149]

Jacinta's devotion to the Immaculate Heart enabled her to love, to pray, and to offer sacrifices for the salvation of souls. This young visionary desired to put that same love and "fire," as she labeled it, "into the hearts of all." Her zeal — indeed her "fire" — are evidence of the Holy Spirit at work in her young heart. She told her cousin, "I so love the Immaculate Heart of Mary! If I could only put into the hearts of all, the fire that is burning within my own heart."[150]

---

[147] Ibid., 314.
[148] Gaitley, *33 Days to Morning Glory*, 76.
[149] Ibid., 60.
[150] Apostoli, *Fatima for Today*, 19.

The Virgin Mary holds the astounding events of the plan of salvation in her humble heart: "Mary kept all these things, pondering them in her heart" (see Luke 2:19). Her role in God's rescue plan has always been to bring Jesus to the world. From the very beginning, our Blessed Mother was about her mission. "She went in haste" and brought the Savior, hidden in her virginal womb, to the home of Elizabeth and Zechariah. The entire plan of salvation involves the heart of Mary through her identity as Mother of the Savior and Mother of the Church — of all of us.

Saint Teresa of Calcutta understood the spiritual power and significance of Mary's heart and with childlike trust asked, "Mary, lend me your Immaculate Heart."[151] She also asked our Blessed Mother to take hers in exchange: "Keep me in your most pure heart."[152] Mother Teresa's life, her ability to love beyond measure, was a gift to the world made possible through the Immaculate Heart of Mary.

We can do the same. It may sound oversimplified and even naive, but if we ask our Heavenly Mother, she will lend us her heart so we can come to love Jesus as we should. In turn, we ought to offer her our hearts, and she will remake them like hers. In this way, we can become single-hearted, "all in," without duplicity. In other words, "pure of heart."[153]

Saint Louis de Montfort tells us that when the Holy Spirit finds his holy spouse, Mary, in a soul, He rushes to that soul to enter it in proportion to the place it has given to her.[154] The Holy

---

[151] Ibid., 75.

[152] Ibid.

[153] "Blessed are the pure in heart, for they shall see God" (see Matt. 5:8).

[154] St. Louis-Marie de Montfort, *True Devotion to the Blessed Virgin* (e-Saint Library, 2010), chap. 1, par. 36, Kindle locations 383–384.

Spirit inhabited, and still does, Mother Teresa's soul, her mission and her work, because He found Mary's heart there.

If we want the Holy Spirit to inhabit us, to make our lives spiritually fruitful and triumphant against the enemy, we should follow Mother Teresa's example and ask our Mother Mary to lend us her heart and to take ours in exchange. One of the most powerful ways to accomplish this is through Marian consecration. Marian consecration means consecrating ourselves to Jesus through Mary. It is all about getting closer to Jesus and the easiest, fastest, most direct way we get there is through His Mother's heart. Those who have done this, in the best sense, are never the same. Giving our hearts to Mary is life changing.[155]

Marian Consecration

The Blessed Virgin Mary's role in God's plan is irreplaceable and necessary. Those who distance themselves from this truth are not in good company. That was Lucifer's position and the reason he was thrown out of heaven. It is believed that when Lucifer was shown that human nature would be joined to divinity through a human woman, he recoiled. He could not accept that a lesser creature would be elevated to a position of queenship over him.[156]

---

[155] Ibid., Kindle locations 1111–1113.

[156] "It is said that God presented Lucifer with a vision of the future: a lesser creature of human nature would be joined to divinity itself, and the Mother of that God-Man would be queen over even the angels. Satan recoiled from such submission; this was the beginning of the enmity between her offspring and his.... In the twelfth chapter of Revelation, Mary is said to be the sign of victory over the forces of evil. The war is not over, of course, until Jesus comes again." Fr. Anselm Romb, O.F.M. Conv., *Total*

People could be in the devil's corner on this matter with good intentions; they might be misinformed or perhaps, through no fault of their own, were brought up in a culture that is hostile toward the Virgin Mary. Although they may be less culpable, they have unknowingly sided with Satan, who will use their misguided allegiance to further his evil agenda. As Christians, we turn away from Mary at our own peril.

The devil does not want us to consecrate ourselves to Jesus through Mary because Marian consecration is the warrior's weapon that leads to the enemy's defeat. Louis de Montfort, a French Catholic priest and Third Order Dominican (1673–1716), understood this. In his *Treatise on the True Devotion to the Blessed Virgin*, Father de Montfort prophesied the devil's attempt to silence the message of Marian consecration. He wrote:

> I clearly foresee that raging beasts will come in fury to tear to pieces with their diabolical teeth this little book.... They will cause it at least to lie hidden in the darkness and silence of a chest and so prevent it from seeing the light of day.[157]

Not surprisingly, Father de Montfort's manuscript, which is an instructional guide to Marian consecration, was hidden in a trunk and discovered by chance in 1842, almost 130 years later! In it, one learns how entrusting ourselves to the Blessed Virgin is not only the surest way to grow in holiness but also a most powerful weapon against the evil one.

Consecration to Mary: Nine-Day Preparation in the Spirit of St. Maximilian Kolbe (Libertyville, IL: Marytown Press, 2006), 91.

[157] De Montfort, *True Devotion to the Blessed Virgin*, Kindle locations 1019–1026.

Almost a century later, during the World War II German occupation of Poland, a Polish seminarian, Karol Wojtyla (1920–2005), came across the little book. Later, as Pope John Paul II, he would write:

> The reading of this book was a decisive turning-point in my life ... which coincided with my clandestine preparation for the priesthood. It was at that time that this curious treatise came into my hands.... I remember carrying it on me for a long time, even at the sodium factory.... I continually went back to certain passages.... As a result, my devotion to the Mother of Christ ... yielded to a new attitude springing from the depths of my faith, as though from the very heart of the Trinity and Jesus Christ ... [158]

Clearly the devil does not want us to be devoted to the Blessed Virgin Mary, and he will discourage us from making the life-altering decision to consecrate ourselves to her. Marianist father and prolific writer Emile Neubert (1878–1967) tells us exactly why Marian consecration is vital to the mission of the Church:

> Since Mary, associated with the Redeemer, has received the mission of destroying the empire of Satan, we must second her action in this task. Hence the filial and apostolic character of this consecration.[159]

---

[158] André Frossard and Pope John Paul II, *Be Not Afraid! Pope John Paul II Speaks Out on His Life, His Beliefs, and His Inspiring Vision for Humanity* (New York: St. Martin's Press, 1984), 125.

[159] Father Emile Neubert, *Life of Union with Mary*, trans. Sylvester P. Juergens, S.M., S.T.D. (New Bedford, MA: Academy of the Immaculate, 2014), 19.

Pope John Paul II tells us that Marian consecration is crucial to our spiritual formation. He writes, "What is more, this 'perfect devotion' [Marian consecration] is indispensable to anyone who means to give himself without reserve to Christ and to the work of redemption."[160]

Consecration is about entrustment. If God the Father entrusted His Son to the Blessed Virgin Mary, we certainly can entrust ourselves to her. Her job is to make us into saints, other Christs for the world. There is no surer way to holiness, no better formation for us than consecration to Our Blessed Mother. This consecration can be a simple heartfelt prayer, or it can be done formally, according to a prescribed rite.

Mothers and fathers can entrust their children to the Blessed Mother. Often, we find that very holy men and women were consecrated by their mothers to our Lady when they were just days old. It is a spiritual strategy of the warrior mother. Young Margaret Bosco did this. We have her testimony from a conversation with her son John before he was ordained:

> When you came into the world, I consecrated you to the Blessed Virgin. When you began your studies, I recommended to you devotion to this Mother of ours. Now I say to you, be completely hers; love those of your companions who have devotion to Mary; and if you become a priest, always preach and promote devotion to Mary.

Since Marian consecration is intended to be a watershed moment in one's life, it is appropriate to take time to prepare for it. There are several authentic preparations that coordinate the day of consecration with a Marian feast and include a similar

---

[160] Ibid.

prayer of entrustment. Louis de Montfort's *Preparation for Total Consecration* is the most well known. Father de Montfort's language can be challenging; it was, after all, written in 1712, and his style is flowery and intense. But its message is magnificent, and modern saints have had recourse to it.

Father Michael Gaitley has given us *33 Days to Morning Glory: A Do-It-Yourself Retreat in Preparation for Marian Consecration.* Father Gaitley's preparation includes a study of four great Marian saints: Louis de Montfort, Mother Teresa, Maximilian Kolbe, and John Paul II.[161]

The Militia Immaculata (MI), established by Maximilian Kolbe, also has a consecration preparation with a specific rite that is performed. The following prayer of entrustment is from the MI's Consecration Prayer for Individuals:

> O Immaculata, Queen of heaven and earth, Refuge of sinners and our most loving Mother, God has willed to entrust the entire order of mercy to you.
>
> I, (name), a repentant sinner, cast myself at your feet humbly imploring you to take me with all that I am and have, wholly to yourself as your possession and property.

---

[161] I went through Father Gaitley's *33 Days to Morning Glory* preparation at my parish, Christ the King in Milwaukie, Oregon, and was consecrated on the Feast of the Assumption of the Blessed Virgin Mary, August 15, 2012. During the preparation, I identified more intensely with Maximilian Kolbe, and so I chose the consecration prayer from the Militia Immaculata. It was a game-changer for me, right up there with getting married and having children. I urge you, dear reader, if you have not been consecrated to Jesus through Mary, to do so. And if you have been consecrated, I encourage you to do a preparation again for a reconsecration on your anniversary feast day.

Please make of me, of all my powers of soul and body, of my whole life, death and eternity, whatever most pleases you. If it please you, use all that I am and have without reserve, wholly to accomplish what was said of you: "She will crush your head," and "You alone have destroyed all the heresies in the world."

Let me be a fit instrument in your immaculate and merciful hands for introducing and increasing your glory to the maximum in all the many strayed and indifferent souls, and thus help extend as far as possible the blessed kingdom of the most Sacred Heart of Jesus. For wherever you enter you obtain the grace of conversion and growth in holiness, since it is through your hands that all graces come to us from the most Sacred Heart of Jesus.[162]

"The most fearful enemy that God has set up against the devil is Mary, his holy Mother."[163] It makes good sense, therefore, to entrust ourselves to her. She is a sure guide and safe haven in this life. If we give ourselves over to her care, she will help us to overcome our faults and grow in virtue and holiness. Like the children of Fatima, Mother Mary will form us into battle-ready warriors.

---

[162] Romb, *Total Consecration*, 94.
[163] De Montfort, *True Devotion to the Blessed Virgin*, Kindle location 515.

14

Humility, Receptivity, and Trust: Requirements for the Battle

Humility

We must be humble, like a child, or we cannot enter heaven (see Matt. 18:1–5). A young child is completely reliant on his or her parents for everything. It is the same for us: we are totally dependent on God. And the amazing paradox is that if we truly humble ourselves like children, we will be the greatest in God's kingdom: quite the opposite of Lucifer,[164] whose rebellious pride cost him Heaven. "The angels too, who did not keep to their own domain but deserted their proper dwelling, he has kept in eternal chains, in gloom, for the judgment of the great day" (Jude 1:6).

Cast down to earth, the devil continues his efforts to bring as many people as he can into rebellion against God. Our Lord explained this to Saint Bridget of Sweden (1303–1373). She writes, "Although the devil lost the dignity of his previous rank [first state], he did not lose his knowledge [cunning], which he

---

[164] Satan's original name, Lucifer, means "light bearer." His words *"Non serviam"* (I will not serve) precipitated his fall.

possesses for the testing of the good and for his own confusion [shame]."[165]

Satan wanted to be like God. He tempted Eve to the same desire,[166] and he wants us also to crave the authority and power that belong only to God. This is pride, the root of all sin and of all disordered desires and behaviors in the world. And it is only through Jesus, the God-Man, that the evil in the world can be eradicated and the world can be re-created, for "the Son of God was revealed to destroy the works of the devil" (1 John 3:8). The Church teaches that Jesus came to help us win this battle:

> The whole of man's history has been the story of our combat with the powers of evil, stretching, so our Lord tells us, from the very dawn of history until the last day (CCC 409).

We on earth are "in the midst of the battlefield" (CCC 409).

If we follow Christ, we will share in His divinity. That is precisely how we become like God. We receive this gift from Jesus; it cannot be seized through prideful disobedience. Because of God's unimaginable humility, the second person of the Blessed Trinity chose to empty Himself of His glory and take on our human nature. At the Incarnation, our Lord was a single-cell zygote in

---

[165] *Saint Bridget's Revelations*, bk. 5, *The Book of Questions*, online version, http://www.catholic-saints.net/saints/st-bridget/st-bridget-book5.php. See also John LaBriola, *Onward Catholic Soldier* (n.p.: Luke 1:38 Publishing, 2008), 16.

[166] "The account of the fall in Genesis 3 uses figurative language, but affirms a primeval event, a deed that took place at the beginning of the history of man. Revelation gives us the certainty of faith that the whole of human history is marked by the original fault freely committed by our first parents" (CCC 390; cf. GS 13 § 1).

the womb of the Virgin Mary, totally dependent on her for His very survival, unseen and seemingly insignificant. This was the first of many revelations of His divine humility. And because of His humble sharing in our human nature, we are invited to share in His divine nature. Humility is the only path to victory.

Teresa of Avila gave us the most concise definition of humility: "Humility is walking in the truth." Simple, but it can be tricky. We first must get to the root of truth. How do we do that?

First, we contemplate our relationship with the Lord. The great Catholic philosopher Dietrich von Hildebrand writes, "It is only in our encounter with a personal God that we become fully aware of our condition as creatures"[167] as well as our beloved place in God's heart. Truth then, is recognizing our total dependence on God. We are creatures; He is the Creator. This humble realization is also an opportunity to discover how precious we are to Him; He loves us to an outrageous degree, proving it by becoming one of us and sacrificing Himself for us.[168]

Second, we reflect on our relationship with others. The humble person understands his or her creaturely equality with others. Everyone has the same dignity given to him or her by God and the same call to live with Him eternally.

Third, we honestly consider ourselves, our inner thoughts and motivations. Humility keeps us from reaching beyond ourselves and "restrains the unruly desire for personal greatness."[169]

Saint Peter, our first pope, counseled:

---

[167] Dietrich von Hildebrand, *Humility: Wellspring of Virtue* (Manchester, NH: Sophia Institute Press, 1997), 24.

[168] "No one has greater love than this, to lay down one's life for one's friends" (John 15:13).

[169] John A. Hardon, S.J. *Pocket Catholic Dictionary* (New York: Image Books, 1985), 183.

Clothe yourselves with humility in your dealings with one another, for: "God opposes the proud but bestows favor on the humble." So humble yourselves under the mighty hand of God, that he may exalt you in due time. (1 Pet. 5:5–6)

In fact, it was Saint Catherine of Siena's humility that freed eight-year-old Lorenza from demonic possession. Catherine's spiritual director, Raymond of Capua, was personally involved, knew the parents of the girl, and confirmed that the child was indeed possessed. He writes:

It was discovered that the evil spirit that was plaguing her (Lorenza) was in the habit of speaking a very elegant form of Latin through her mouth (despite the fact that the child knew nothing about the language), and could solve deep and difficult problems and reveal the sins and state of conscience of particular individuals.[170]

Previously repeated efforts to free the child had failed. It was only through humility that Catherine was able to force the demon out of the girl. Raymond of Capua continues:

After a long struggle, realizing that he [the evil spirit] would be forced to leave Lorenza, he said, "If I come out of here I will enter into you." Immediately the virgin [Catherine] replied, "If the Lord wills it so, and I know that without His permission you can do nothing, God forbid that I should prevent you, or in any other way alienate myself from His Will or set myself up against

---

[170] Raymond of Capua, *The Life of St. Catherine of Siena by Her Confessor* (Charlotte, NC: TAN Books, 2011), 217.

Him." Whereupon the proud spirit, struck amidships by such humility, lost nearly all the power he had over the little girl.[171]

Humility is essential; this foundational virtue disposes us for our role in the human struggle against the powers of evil. We cannot outmaneuver or outsmart Satan on our own. The demons are pure spirit with an intellect far superior to ours. They've been around human beings since the beginning, studying us unceasingly, and therefore, they know how best to ensnare us. Saint Vincent de Paul offers us excellent guidance in our dealings with the devil:

> The most powerful weapon to conquer the devil is humility. For as he does not know at all how to employ it, neither does he know how to defend himself from it.[172]

Receptivity

Make no mistake about it, every woman is "wired" for receptivity. Women, naturally, have a predisposition to this most desirable attribute. We may not recognize it; our receptive nature may be buried deep within us. It may be distorted by woundedness, sin, or an incorrect understanding; but it is there.

Consider the analogy of receptivity in the natural world and the spiritual world. When the Church brings souls into the kingdom of God, it is a spiritual birth. The Church must first receive grace from God. If she cooperates with that grace, the Church gives back to God new members of the Body of

[171] Ibid., 221.
[172] Esper, *Saintly Solutions*, 261.

Christ: spiritual children.[173] The Church cannot *take* grace from God; she must *receive* it and cooperate with it in order to bring this spiritual life to others. Analogous to the Church, a woman's body is receptive in order to bring forth physical life. The Catholic philosopher Alice von Hildebrand comments on the woman's body:

> The greatness of her role is illustrated by the fact that she is given but a microscopic seed; she gives back a human being, made to God's image and likeness.[174]

Receptivity is the state of being available and open for what God wants to do in and through us. In this way it is not mere passivity or inertness. Receptivity is active and dynamic. In no way does receptivity deprive us of our personalities or render us weak and ineffective. The opposite is true. Our acknowledgment and cultivation of this gift of femininity enhances our entire selves. Receptivity is a dying to self-determination and paradoxically, an embracing of our truest self. The activity—the "doing" flows from God's action within the receptive woman. There is a right order to the productivity of God's saving work in this world: receptivity comes first. And it is a powerful feminine weapon in the battle to save souls.

Everything the Church Militant does is for the salvation of souls. But saving souls from what? Our Lord sacrificed His life for us, dying a horrific, humiliating death, suffering beyond

---

[173] In this way, men, as members of the Church, are to be receptive, too, although this attribute is not prominent in men, as it is in women.

[174] Alice von Hildebrand, Ph.D., "The Privilege of Being a Woman," in *Real Women*, ed. Sr. Concetta Belleggia D.S.P. (San Francisco: Ignatius Press, 1994), 19.

comprehension, precisely because there is a hell to save us from. Jesus warned us repeatedly about hell:

> Thus it will be at the end of the age. The angels will go out and separate the wicked from the righteous and throw them into the fiery furnace, where there will be wailing and grinding of teeth. (Matt. 13:49–50)

There is a lot at stake. The Fatima children were shown hell. Our Lady told them that many souls fall into hell because they have no one to pray for them. The Lord Jesus did much the same for Saint Faustina. She writes:

> Today, I was led by an Angel to the chasms of hell.... I would have died at the very sight of these tortures if the omnipotence of God had not supported me.... I, Sister Faustina, by the order of God, have visited the abysses of hell so that I might tell souls about it and testify to its existence.... What I have written is but a pale shadow of the things I saw. But I noticed one thing: that most of the souls there are those who disbelieved that there is a hell.[175]

Every human person will live forever in heaven or in hell. This is what the war with the eternal foe is all about — our eternal destinies. The devil wants us and the souls of our families, our spouses, our children, our grandchildren, and our friends. This is why we need to nurture receptivity in ourselves. The evil one would have us disdain that which serves the Kingdom of God and reject our feminine nature.

Our example par excellence is the Virgin Mary. When the angel came to her at the Annunciation, she was absolutely available

---

[175] Saint Maria Faustina Kowalska, *Diary*, no. 741.

to God, without exception. She trusted Him completely. Being found pregnant before she and Joseph were living together as husband and wife would have presented a potentially dangerous situation. God's rescue mission for all humanity required one woman's receptive yes, Mary's fiat, and she responded without hesitation, "Behold, I am the handmaid of the Lord. May it be done to me according to your word" (Luke 1:38).

Receptivity is not passivity. Receptivity actively cooperates with God and, by doing so, contributes to accomplishing God's will. Our Blessed Mother demonstrates this when she launches Jesus' public ministry at the wedding at Cana. There, He addresses her as "woman," referring to "the woman" and her seed (both of them), who will crush the head of the serpent (Gen. 3:15). She advances His mission, which includes His Passion and death, and "a sword will pierce" her heart as well (Luke 2:35). Mary is receptive and trusting without reservation as she embraces her role in the plan of salvation.

If we are to become the women we were created to be, effective warriors in this cosmic battle, we must be humble and cultivate holy receptivity.

Trust

Below the image of Divine Mercy are the words "Jesus, I trust in You." In the Divine Mercy message, Jesus repeatedly makes known His desire that we trust Him. Our lack of trust wounds His heart more than other sins: "My child, all your sins have not wounded My Heart as painfully as your present lack of trust does."[176]

---

[176] Ibid., no. 1486.

As mentioned earlier, lack of trust led our first parents to sin. The devil approached Eve and planted doubt in her mind (Gen. 3:1–6). Eve thought God was keeping something from her and Adam; she did not trust in His goodness. In the face of the lie of a fallen angel, the serpent, Eve made her choice. Eve's lack of trust, and Adam's for that matter, plunged humanity into sin.

The theme of trust appears again at the turning point of salvation history. At the Incarnation, the Blessed Virgin Mary responds with total trust. The rescue plan for humanity is put into play with her fiat.

Trust must be distinguished from the sin of presumption. Assuming that, regardless of one's decisions and actions, one will automatically go to heaven because God is merciful is the sin of presumption. This mind-set dominates today's culture, and it is based on a misunderstanding of God's mercy.

Presumption lends itself to ingratitude and an entitlement attitude. Presumptuous people take Jesus for granted and are not grateful for all that God has done for them. They use others without the investment of a genuine relationship.

Trust is very different. If we trust someone, we will do what that person says. For instance, if a person whom we trust ran into a room and shouted, "Get out of the building now!" we would do it and do it quickly. If we trust Jesus, we will do what He says. He tells us, "Whoever wishes to come after me must deny himself, take up his cross, and follow me" (Matt. 16:24). Trusting Jesus is the most important thing we can do in this life. Trust is powerful. Consider that Jesus Christ, the Second Person of the Holy Trinity, is, in a sense, held captive by our trust. Our Lord explained to Faustina:

> Your great trust in Me forces Me to continuously grant you graces. You have great and incomprehensible rights

over My Heart, for you are a daughter of complete trust.[177]

In the ongoing fight for souls, the Christian warrior understands that she must trust Jesus; there is simply no other way to engage the enemy with any hope of victory. We must follow the examples of the Blessed Virgin and of Saint Faustina and, like them, become daughters who trust completely.[178]

[177] Ibid., no. 718.
[178] Ibid.

15

Who Are You?

This book has presented, for the most part, women saints doing many things. In a certain sense, the premise of this work is a call to action. But there is an order that must be respected. Our identity in Christ comes first. We must know ourselves, who we are created to be, before we grab our sword and head for the battlefield. "Being" comes before "doing."

So, who are you? You are a child of God. You have always been in the mind of God. He anticipated your arrival on earth and the eternity you are destined to share with Him. You exist because God the Father thought of you and willed your existence. No matter what your circumstances are, you were wanted and are loved by God. Your value is infinite, and it comes only from God. Before you were conceived, God knew everything about you: "You formed my inmost being; you knit me in my mother's womb" (Ps. 139:13). The Lord understood the challenges you would face and the circumstances of your life. And He has a plan for your life, "For I know well the plans I have in mind for you ... plans for your welfare and not for woe, so as to give you a future of hope" (Jer. 29:11).

No matter what path you've taken to this point in your life, no matter what you have done or what has happened to you, there's no situation, no event, no sin that can change the fact that God loves you and desires your friendship. We are transformed in our familial connection with Jesus, as adopted children of God. It is where we are healed and become our true selves.

If you give Jesus your life, starting with forgiveness, He will draw goodness out of your past, no matter how wounded, convoluted, idyllic, or sinful. Your life, all of it, becomes part of your personal salvation history. Jesus is the Divine Physician. He waits for us in the sacrament of Penance, where the devil trembles before His mercy. He told St. Faustina, "When a soul extols My goodness [in the confessional], Satan trembles before it and flees to the very bottom of hell."[179]

Like His forefather King David, Jesus is a warrior king. But unlike David, King Jesus battles for souls, and "his kingdom will have no end."[180] Through Baptism, we have been grafted onto the Body of Christ. We are therefore royalty by adoption, and like our king, we are also warriors. He came to do battle with our enemy: "The Son of God came into the world to destroy the works of the devil" (see 1 John 3:8). And Jesus desires that we participate in His saving work and, with Him, enter the battle for souls. He shares His divine plans with us:

> I no longer call you slaves, because a slave does not know what his master is doing. I have called you friends, because I have told you everything I have heard from my Father. (John 15:15)

You can absolutely trust God, no matter how things appear. The safest place you can possibly be is in His will. Hold tightly

---

[179] Ibid., no. 378.
[180] Nicene Creed.

to your true identity. Jesus did. Even though He hung on the Cross as a convicted criminal, Jesus knew He could trust His Father. Despite how it appeared, the Cross was the most perfect place for Him to be; His identity as the beloved Son remained throughout.

In battle, there are those who will be called to give the ultimate witness by laying down their lives. More often, though, we are called to share in Christ's redemption of the world through a different kind of martyrdom: a death to our own will and desires. And from the perspective of the world, which tells us to put ourselves first, we appear defeated. But that is not the truth. As with the Cross, what appears to be a defeat is victory in Christ. Jesus assures us, "I have told you this so that you might have peace in me. In the world you will have trouble, but take courage, I have conquered the world" (John 16:33).

The devil does not want you to know the dignity, power, and reality of being a child of God and your call to share in our Lord's divine nature and to join Jesus on the battlefield for souls. And so, the evil one has filled the world with confusion about what it means to be human. He wants you to reject your birthright and settle for half-truths, distorted truths, and fascinating substitutes. But nothing will satisfy except God and His plan for you.

You can really trust Jesus to complete the work He started in you. He has a magnificent vision for your life that, with your cooperation, will be realized. And our Lord honors your desire to trust Him, even if you trust imperfectly. The saint is not a person who gets perfection right on the first try. Rather, the saint is the person who never quits; who falls and gets up, over and over again.

Know this: the devil fears your yes to God. Why? Because he knows that the Queen of Heaven and Earth is your mother and if you join your fiat to hers, it has the power to crush the head of the serpent.

You landed in this particular day and time by God's design; it is part of His plan. Your yes to God's unique will for your life has an impact on eternity. Give yourself completely to the identity that God has for you; this is how the battle is waged and how it is won. Allow Him to show you your true worth! Receive His vision for you. And as you make your way through life in this fallen world, always hold tightly to your position as a child of God. You are, after all, the offspring of *the Woman*, one who follows Christ and wages war with the devil.

About the Author

Julie Onderko and her husband, Tom, reside in Milwaukie, Oregon. They have three grown sons and seven grandchildren. Julie is the coordinator of evangelization at her parish, Christ the King Catholic Church. Julie hosts a weekly podcast and radio show through Mater Dei Radio titled *Your Next Mission from God*. She is a Catholic speaker and leader of retreats and seminars. Julie earned a master of arts in theology at the Augustine Institute.

Sophia Institute

Sophia Institute is a nonprofit institution that seeks to nurture the spiritual, moral, and cultural life of souls and to spread the Gospel of Christ in conformity with the authentic teachings of the Roman Catholic Church.

Sophia Institute Press fulfills this mission by offering translations, reprints, and new publications that afford readers a rich source of the enduring wisdom of mankind.

Sophia Institute also operates the popular online resource CatholicExchange.com. *Catholic Exchange* provides world news from a Catholic perspective as well as daily devotionals and articles that will help readers to grow in holiness and live a life consistent with the teachings of the Church.

In 2013, Sophia Institute launched Sophia Institute for Teachers to renew and rebuild Catholic culture through service to Catholic education. With the goal of nurturing the spiritual, moral, and cultural life of souls, and an abiding respect for the role and work of teachers, we strive to provide materials and programs that are at once enlightening to the mind and ennobling to the heart; faithful and complete, as well as useful and practical.

Sophia Institute gratefully recognizes the Solidarity Association for preserving and encouraging the growth of our apostolate over the course of many years. Without their generous and timely support, this book would not be in your hands.

www.SophiaInstitute.com
www.CatholicExchange.com
www.SophiaInstituteforTeachers.org

Sophia Institute Press® is a registered trademark of Sophia Institute. Sophia Institute is a tax-exempt institution as defined by the Internal Revenue Code, Section 501(c)(3). Tax ID 22-2548708.